Miss Fatty Cat's Revenge

Meg Welch Dendler

Cats in the Mirror Series

Book 1: *Why Kimba Saved The World*

Book 2: *Vacation Hiro*

Book 3: *Miss Fatty Cat's Revenge*

Book 4: *Slinky Steps Out*

Book 5: *Kimba's Christmas*

And the Companion Books

Max's Wild Night

Dottie's Daring Day

Also by Meg Welch Dendler

Bianca: The Brave Frail and Delicate Princess

Bianca: Journey to Ryuugito

For Older Readers

At the Corner of Magnetic and Main

The Tigran Chronicles

Published by Serenity Mountain Publishing

Springdale, AR

Miss Fatty Cat's Revenge

©2014 by Meg Welch Dendler.

All rights reserved.

www.megdendler.com

Second Edition, 2019

ISBN: 978-1733645003

Cover design by Lesley Hollinger Vernon. Adapted for Second Edition by Kelsey Rice.

Photos of Karma, Brady, Willy, and Bam Bam courtesy of Turpentine Creek Wildlife Refuge.

Photos of Medusa provided by Lilah Stiger. Other photos by Scott or Meg Dendler.

No part of this book, text or photos, may be copied, reproduced, or shared in any form without the written consent of the author. All copyright laws apply.

 Created with Vellum

Contents

Preface	ix
Some cats . . .	xi
So Far in the Series	xiii

Chapter 1 — 1
NIGHTTIME SONG

Chapter 2 — 5
A NEW HOUSE

Chapter 3 — 18
FUR TRACES

Chapter 4 — 26
BLUE-RIBBON SPECIAL AGENT

Chapter 5 — 33
CRABBY FATTY CAT

Chapter 6 — 41
AN UNAUTHORIZED TRANSFER

Chapter 7 — 50
KARMA

Chapter 8 — 61
HORUS IS UNIMPRESSED

Chapter 9 — 65
LIONS AND TIGERS AND BEARS

Chapter 10 — 75
WHAT SLINKY SAW

Chapter 11 — 81
TRACING THE TRANSFER

Chapter 12 — 89
ALONE

Chapter 13 *TRAITOR IN OUR RANKS*	93
Chapter 14 *THOTH'S BAD NEWS*	100
Chapter 15 *TRUSTED ALLIES*	108
Chapter 16 *DISTURBED SLEEP*	116
Chapter 17 *WHERE'S KIMBA?*	122
Chapter 18 *OPERATION REFUGE RESCUE*	132
Chapter 19 *BUDDY TO THE RESCUE*	147
Chapter 20 *HELPFUL HUMANS*	158
Chapter 21 *THE PENALTY FOR TREASON*	167
Chapter 22 *MEDUSA AND KIMBA*	180
Chapter 23 *HOME AGAIN*	186
Chapter 24 *OPERATION OZARK OCCUPATION*	194
Sample Chapter of Slinky Steps Out	199
Slinky Steps Out, Chapter 1 *MOVING BOXES*	200

Cats in the Mirror Series	207
Companion Books	209
Also by Meg Welch Dendler	211
For Older Readers	213
Review Request	215
Author's Note	217
Gratitude	223
Photo of Miss Fatty Cat	225
Words You May Not Know	227
Photo of Miss Fatty Cat	247
About the Author	249

The characters and events in this book
are not based on real events.
Well, maybe a little bit.
But the names have been changed
to protect the innocent.
Sometimes.

All of the stories in this series are full of real events in the lives of our cats Kimba and Hiro. You will find photos of them at the end of many chapters, as well as photos of other cats and events that sparked my imagination.

Of course, Kimba and Hiro don't really talk to alien cats in our bathroom mirror, nor do they visit ships in space. Not that I've ever seen. Maybe they are just tricky.

You never know with cats.

Some cats are born on Earth
and never know who they really are.
Others are sent.
They are undercover for their years on Earth.
They know who they are.
They know that they are not from Earth at all.
And they are part of a bigger plan.

So Far in the Series

In Book 1, *Why Kimba Saved The World*, Kimba and Hiro were found by Mama and Daddy as abandoned two-day-old kittens. They were rescued, and they joined the family along with the human children, Mindy and Leia, and their cats, Miss Fatty Cat and Slinky. The outdoor cat, Buddy, and The Big Black Beast also lived there.

Quite by accident, Kimba and Hiro discovered that alien cats were watching them through the bathroom mirror. These Cats in the Mirror live on a spaceship close to Earth. Kimba was excited to complete missions that were assigned to her from her alien contact, Special Agent Regalus.

At first, it was fun and made her feel important.

But then Kimba realized that Regalus had her wrapped up in a plot to help the alien cats invade Earth through the humans' Facebook pages.

Fearing for the safety of her human family, Kimba did not follow through on the Facebook mission. Other cats on Earth failed to cooperate too. The invasion was a failure, and Kimba and Hiro decided to stop talking to the Cats in the Mirror forever.

In Book 2, *Vacation Hiro*, the family left for a week-long vacation. Hiro accidentally began talking with the Cats in the Mirror again. This time their contact was Special Agent Artemis.

Artemis did not have missions for the cats, but he revealed to them that they were not just ordinary cats. Kimba and Hiro were the daughters of High Commander Felicity and Commander Griffin.

They were unexpectedly born on Earth while their mother was on a mission. They were separated from her when the human Daddy found them. Their cat parents allowed them to stay hidden away in their Earth home. The Cats in the Mirror monitored their safety at all times.

Kimba and Hiro also learned that alien cats have been coming to Earth for millions of years. Saber-tooth cats, lions, tigers, and cats of every shape and size came from different groups of space-traveling felines.

Cats on the spaceships lived in a very structured society. Family rank and value were important. The rank of high commander was inherited, and only certain cat families could become special agents. Kimba and Hiro learned that they were like royalty in the alien cat society.

A rebel group, who was impressed with the democratic election process on Earth, wanted to change things on the ships. They were making life very difficult for Felicity and Griffin. The rebels might want to harm Kimba and Hiro as a part of their plans for changing the system.

Kimba and Hiro had a chance to visit the spaceship and learn about their cat family. They experienced the transfer process that allowed alien cats to travel between Earth and the ship.

In the end, they returned to their human family on Earth to spend a small portion of the hundreds of years a cat can actually live. This is called an Earth-life. After fifteen years or so, Kimba and Hiro expected to have their life essence transferred back to the ship, where their lives as part of the family of highest-ranking cats in existence would begin.

Miss Fatty Cat and Slinky were also alien cats enjoying an Earth-life, though they denied knowing anything about the Cats in the Mirror to Kimba and Hiro. Miss Fatty Cat was jealous of the attention that Kimba and Hiro received from the human family. She teamed up with one of the rebel alien cats to help get rid of them.

What does Miss Fatty Cat have in store for Kimba and Hiro? Find out in Book 3: *Miss Fatty Cat's Revenge*.

Miss Fatty Cat was once a skinny baby kitten. She got over that very soon, but she always had a lot to say about everything.

Chapter 1
NIGHTTIME SONG

Kimba, the stealthy hunter, crept between the sleeping bodies. Not one of them sensed her presence. Choosing the perfect victim, she took hold of his throat. She lifted her prey carefully so his cries did not wake the others. The tiny pig in the striped sweater was now helpless in her clutches. Kimba slipped away and began her victory song as she climbed the steep mountain to rejoin her family.

"I have won!" she sang loud and clear. "The victory is mine. The pig is dead. Hurrah for Kimba!"

"Yes, Kimba, we hear you. You are a mighty hunter," Mama mumbled from behind the bedroom door. "Now go back to sleep."

Kimba dropped her prize outside the door and

began washing her front toes in frustration. If Mama were really impressed, she would have opened the door to admire her Kimba Baby's hard work.

Humans just don't understand the skill it takes to be a master hunter, she thought sadly.

In the old house, it was a quick trip from the toy collection on Mama's office shelves to the bedroom door. In this new house, it now required lugging her victim up a tall staircase. Some appreciation would be nice. She sang a few extra forlorn notes, just to make sure Mama understood.

"Herrrow, herrrow, merrrrow!"

In the room next door, Miss Fatty Cat was snoring, belly-up on Leia's bed. Kimba's nightly routine disturbed her sleep, and she rolled onto her side with a loud snort. Leia groaned and pulled the blankets up over her head. All of the nighttime hunting and singing was nothing new, but Leia's room used to be far away from the adults. The girl and her cat slept through it. Not in this strange new house.

Stupid cat, sing while you can, Miss Fatty Cat thought. *Your time is coming.*

SPECIAL AGENT ARTEMIS paced back and forth outside the door of the High Council chamber. It had been over a week since Felicity's daughters had vanished without a trace. The new agent monitoring them during the daytime didn't understand what it meant when strange men took furniture from the bedroom. The packing was over before Artemis came back to his station.

Watching the video playback, Artemis felt a chill run along his spine. The family had moved, and he had no idea where to begin looking for the sisters who were supposed to be under his watchful eye.

Kimba and Hiro were gone, but he would not rest until he found them.

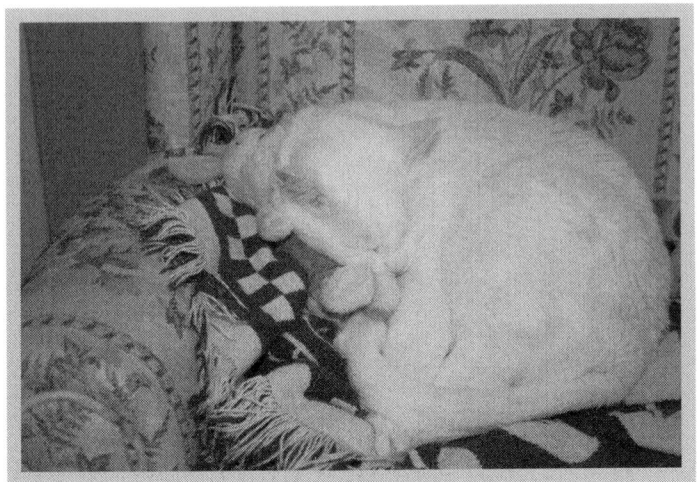

**Kimba loved to hunt toys from Mama's office.
Piglet was one of her favorites.**

Chapter 2
A NEW HOUSE

The day began just like most days in the old house. Daddy was the first one up. He fed The Big Black Beast, but instead of letting him into a fenced backyard, Daddy now spent a long time playing and throwing a ball for The Beast in a huge new yard. Kimba couldn't see a fence out of any window in the house. She watched through the kitchen window screen as The Beast yelped and jumped around, as big a fool as ever.

The summer sun was getting higher in the sky and warmer, but no day in this new house had been as suffocatingly hot as the ones before the move. Kimba remembered the day she was under orders from Regalus and had escaped from the house. She'd ended up stuck outside in the Texas summer heat. She flexed her toes, thinking about the burning-hot driveway and the pokey grass. Here in this new place, the breeze blew warm but peaceful.

The air here smelled different too. No wood chips and live oak trees like before, but lots of grass and always the faint smell of animals she did not recognize. If the wind blew from the open space across from the house, there was a strong odor of poop. Lots of poop.

There must be a giant litter box over there somewhere with bunches of animals sharing it, she thought.

Mama staggered out of the bedroom next, lazily picking up last night's kill.

"Poor Piglet." She sighed. "He never saw it coming. Good morning, Kimba." She waved sleepily toward the window.

Mama made some Ovaltine for breakfast and headed down the steep basement stairs to her new office, Piglet tucked under one arm. Kimba considered following her, but she decided to wait. Mama spent a lot more time in her office now, and there was no rush.

Once Daddy came back inside, he poured food into the cats' feeder dish and made sure the water in the bowl was fresh. Of course, Kimba and Hiro didn't like to drink from the shared bowl. Kimba reminded Daddy of this obvious fact with a quick mew.

"Okay, okay," he said and turned on a gentle stream of water at the kitchen sink so Kimba could get a sip. "Such a spoiled Kimba Baby."

She blinked slowly in return and leaned in. *Lap, lap, lap.* Kimba used the rough spikes on her tongue to catch the water as it ran by. It tasted different here and took some getting used to, but she was happy as long as she didn't have to share with Miss Fatty Cat and Slinky.

Another big change at this house was that no one put food outside for Buddy. He was the wild old cat who used to guard the front yard. As a matter of fact, Kimba and Hiro weren't sure whether he had come with the family at all. In the craziness of those moving days, the sisters had lost track of many things. Buddy was one of them.

Too bad they didn't leave Miss Fatty Cat behind too, Kimba thought as the fat cat waddled past the kitchen and straight to the food bowl in the new mudroom. To get her food at this new house, she jump up on a special counter that was out of reach of the munching teeth of The Big Black Beast. *Hop on up there. It's probably the only exercise you will get all day*, Kimba grumbled to herself.

Finished with her morning drink, Kimba jumped from the kitchen counter and sauntered into Mama and Daddy's bedroom to look for Hiro. She found her in the usual spot, crunching on her private breakfast on the bathroom counter. Kimba nimbly leapt up next to her. She glanced at the huge mirror hanging over the double sinks.

"Anything today?" she asked.

"Nope, not a peep," Hiro mumbled, her mouth full of food.

If Artemis knew where they were, he would have made contact by now. It was odd and a little scary to think they were cut off from the ship and the protective, ever-present blue eyes of the Siamese cat.

"He must be going crazy," Kimba said. "I would have warned him if I knew what was going to happen."

Hiro nodded, and her tail thrashed. Neither of them had understood the signs of "moving." They had gotten lazy about paying attention to the humans' conversations. Thinking back, the sisters should have known something strange was going on.

There had been lots of boxes and cleaning out of closets, but Mama often did projects like that to clear away items the girls had outgrown. Then she donated them to charity. The rest of it had been one big game.

Shredded newspaper was EVERYWHERE! Kimba and Hiro spent hours batting around stray pieces and jumping in and out of boxes full of the crinkly, delightful stuff. Mama would shoo them to away, but that just encouraged the fun. Cabinets were left open for exploring, and boxes stacked high in the corners became excellent sleeping ledges. None of the cats had wondered why. None of them understood what packing meant.

Then came the morning when all of the cats, even the terrified Slinky, found themselves rudely locked in the small guest bathroom. For hours, the four of them listened in horror as strange men clomped through the house in huge work boots and took everything away.

Slinky wedged herself as far back behind the

toilet as she could go. Hiro huddled under the sink with her back twitching and her tail thrashing. She was too upset to chase it. Miss Fatty Cat inched herself into a corner and glared at everyone, as if she knew this craziness was all Kimba and Hiro's fault. Hoping for answers, Kimba leapt up into the small sink and yelled at the decorative mirror hanging there.

"Greetings, Artemis! Something is very wrong! Something is happening!"

The black cat sisters watched with wide eyes, but she didn't care what Miss Fatty Cat and Slinky saw. She yelled and yelled. No one was listening. There had never been a reason to monitor that mirror in the house. Realizing it was hopeless, Kimba had eventually joined the other cats hunkered on the floor. Just as when she was a kitten, Kimba was faced with a big white door that blocked her freedom.

"The top comes off my desk, but leave the computers. They will go in the cars with us," Mama told the strangers.

The cats could smell Daddy and Mindy and Leia walking past the door from time to time. After several hours, everyone but Kimba drifted off to sleep. The white cat stayed alert. Her ears and nose flushed a bright pink, sneezing at the dust blowing under the bathroom door. Throughout the house, she could hear the vacuum cleaner running and muffled voices. Finally, the front door was shut, and the deadbolt was thrown into place for the first time since breakfast.

"Pssssst. Hey," Kimba alerted the others, "it sounds like it's over."

The four cats waited in terror to see what would come next.

"Max's crate is already in the van. Go ahead and take him for a quick walk while I get the cats ready."

Mama's voice sounded strange in the big empty house. It echoed off the tile floors in the kitchen. The cats just stared at the door, ready to dash out the minute it was opened. But Mama was ready for them. She opened it just a crack and then gently nudged with her foot to scare the captives back. Kimba almost made a leap for it over her leg, but Mama blocked her. Then she closed the door and all five of them were in the tiny bathroom together.

Mama had a small orange bottle in her hand. She sat down against the door, opened the bottle, and pulled the struggling Hiro onto her lap. In one quick move, Mama slipped a little white pill into Hiro's mouth and held it closed. Then she rubbed along the top of the tuxedo cat's nose and whispered to her. Kimba jumped into the sink so she could see what was happening.

"It's okay. Just swallow that, and you won't have to worry about anything else for the rest of the day."

Hiro swallowed it, and Mama released her. Slinky was next, so exhausted from the morning of terror that she didn't fight at all. Then came Miss Fatty Cat, too lazy to fight. Once the fat cat was released and ran to the far side of the room, Mama looked up at Kimba. The white cat stared down at her.

"Hmmm," Mama said. "This should be interesting. Maybe I should have brought gloves."

Kneeling next to the sink, she grabbed Kimba's head, forced her mouth open on the sides with two fingers, popped the pill inside, and clamped the cat's mouth shut again.

Kimba fought valiantly. She tried to claw her way free, but Mama held her down with her other arm. The cat scratched at the sink in vain. With all the force she could muster, Kimba managed to spit the bitter pill out. Mama just stuck it back in again.

Kimba couldn't imagine why Mama was doing such a horrible thing to her. It was worse than a trip to the vet. Well, maybe not that bad. The vet had big, sharp needles, and Mama only had a yucky pill. Kimba caught a glance at Miss Fatty Cat out of the corner of her eye and thought she looked rather pleased with the white cat's plight.

"It's not that bad, you silly girl," Mama cooed.

Kimba disagreed. After the longest minute of her life, Kimba swallowed. It was a reflex she couldn't control. Mama checked her mouth to make sure the pill was gone and then let her go. Kimba glared at the woman from the sink. Could this day get any worse?

That was difficult for any of the cats to answer because everything was a little fuzzy after that.

Mama left them in the bathroom again for a few minutes. Kimba was sort of awake when Daddy opened the door, but she couldn't move. It was a weird sensation. He tenderly picked up each of the cats and placed them on blankets inside separate travel carriers. Hiro may not have been able to move much, but she could still yell. And yell she did. Daddy chuckled and whispered to her.

"It will all be over soon. Don't worry. Everything is fine."

The rest of the day was a blur. There was a constant rumbling sound that Kimba recognized as Mama's car. Sometimes there was music playing. Sometimes she could hear Mama and Leia talking. Most of the time she could hear Hiro's faint cries.

At one point, Kimba woke up to find that the car was stopped. Craning her neck with all of her might, Kimba could see out the car window through the side of her carrier. A large car-like thing was next to them. She saw Daddy loading The Big Black Beast into his crate through the side of the machine. Then everything faded out again.

It must have been hours and hours later when Kimba awoke. She was not in the car anymore, and the door to her carrier was open. She could sense the other cats around her, but there were unfamiliar smells in the room. She could move, so Kimba crawled out and took a look around.

The four cats were in a large room with a bathroom attached to it. It was sort of like Mama and Daddy's room at the old house, but there was no furniture. The floors were slippery and hard instead of soft and carpeted.

Peering in the other crates, she noticed that Slinky

was awake, but she was hiding in the back. Miss Fatty Cat and Hiro were still asleep. Kimba leaned in and licked the top of Hiro's head. Her sister responded with a hoarse cry. Just then, Mama walked into the big room.

"Look who's up," she sang. "What do you think of our new house, Kimba Baby?"

New house? Why in the world did we need a new house?

Mama set up a big airbed on the floor for her and Daddy to sleep on. Then she opened up a suitcase filled with clothes. Kimba was weary but climbed inside and nestled down into the familiar scents. It smelled like home. This new place most certainly did not.

"Oh, Kim." Mama laughed, but she let her stay. The woman moved into the bathroom and began to unload items from another bag into the empty cupboards. "You'll see. This new house is going to be great once all of our things arrive."

Kimba highly doubted it, but she was too groggy to argue.

The furniture had arrived—after another horrifying day of being locked in the bathroom. Kimba could admit that the new house was not as bad as she had thought. There were hundreds of birds to watch through the much larger windows.

The outside world around the house was completely different from their city neighborhood. Kimba couldn't even see another house from any of the windows. There were just trees and what Mama called mountains.

Slinky was happy because she and Mindy had a special room in the basement that was separate from all of the household activity. The skinny cat could hide all day, and no one bothered her. The rest of their daily routines fell into place just as easily.

The only difference was that now there were no Cats in the Mirror. From the smell of the house, no other cats had ever lived there. There was no reason for an agent to be watching.

Looking into the large mirror that morning, Kimba saw only her own reflection.

"How in the world will Artemis and our parents find us?" she asked Hiro.

"What if they never do?"

IN LEIA'S BATHROOM, Miss Fatty Cat struggled to keep her balance on the edge of the sink.

"Greetings," she called out, straining to see in the mirror. "Are you there?"

She had been so close to getting rid of the spoiled sisters. Now everything was ruined.

"Hello? Is anyone monitoring this mirror?"

Her cries went unanswered.

Kimba loved sitting in the open windows, watching the hummingbirds and butterflies.

Chapter 3
FUR TRACES

After hours of waiting, exhaustion had forced Special Agent Artemis to return to his room. A cat can only keep his eyes open for so long. The beeping, flashing red light from his computer woke him from an agitated sleep. He slammed his paw down on the button, claws drawn.

"Yes? Did you find them?"

He was greeted by a longhaired white cat with a flat face and bright-green eyes. His ears were perked and at attention.

"Yes, sir. Well, we have found one of their humans. Kimba's fur registration was picked up by the security mirrors in a small-town grocery store in

Northwest Arkansas. Surveillance videos show the human female shopping there."

"Arkansas?" Artemis repeated, licking the back of his paw and rubbing the sleep from his eyes. "Do we have any agents in Arkansas?"

"The high commander knows of one in particular, sir."

"Excellent. Thank you . . . um . . . I don't know that we have worked together before, Special Agent...?"

"Senior Transfer Operations Specialist Snowball, sir."

"Snowball?" Artemis's eyes narrowed. That was not the type of name ship cats usually gave to their children, and only agent-level cats were allowed time on Earth.

"Yes, sir," he replied, tilting his head and looking down. "My parents are fascinated with Earth culture and chose to give all their children traditional human-style names."

Artemis considered the white ball of fluff staring back at him from the computer screen. *Snowball, indeed*, he thought.

"Fine then. But what is a senior transfer operations specialist doing involved in this case?"

Snowball shifted in his seat, and his ears twitched.

"Commander Griffin was willing to accept all available hands-on-deck to find his children as soon as possible. I have taken some training courses on using the mirror-to-mirror communications devices and offered to help."

"I see. Well then, continue the search and let me know if you can confirm any other sightings of their humans."

"Yes, sir. I will keep you informed."

Artemis closed the communication window and sighed in relief. At least the humans had been found. He hoped Kimba and Hiro were still in their care. He couldn't imagine those particular humans had left the sisters behind at an animal shelter or humane society. That happened time and again when humans moved.

Kimba and Hiro's humans were far too attached to their cats to just abandon them, but the sooner he could confirm the sisters' safety, the better. Artemis rushed through his breakfast and bath so he could join in the search.

On his end of the monitor, Snowball sighed as well. That had gone smoothly. In their excitement to find the overly fussed-about sisters, no one had questioned his ability to use the communication portals or what he might do with open access to all of them.

Snowball's whiskers tensed with excitement as he turned his chair to face the dark headquarters control room behind him.

Dozens of computers were hacking into the mirrors of every household in a ten-mile radius of the store where the human female had been spotted. They could see into the bathrooms and bedrooms and living rooms where each mirror hung. One of them would eventually find Kimba and Hiro. That lucky agent would report it directly to Snowball, expecting him to pass the news on to the High Command.

If he could reestablish contact with Agent Ebony before Artemis found the royal sisters, the League For Cat Equality could begin their plan immediately. Satisfied purrs rumbled up from deep inside his chest.

Kimba and Hiro agreed to take shifts. One or the other of them always stayed in range of the bathroom mirror. Hiro was grateful Mama had set up her big pillow bed right across from the bathroom door, on top of the large cedar chest.

From her bed, Hiro could see if anyone showed up in the mirror, and anyone looking through the mirror could see her. It was perfect. Keeping one ear on alert, Hiro napped through the morning.

The humans were bustling around, unpacking boxes and making a dusty mess in every room of the new house. It would be difficult to talk with a Cat in the Mirror for now, but at least Artemis or another agent would be able to see her.

Kimba wandered in after lunch, exhausted from a morning of play. There were empty boxes and big sheets of paper and shredded newspaper everywhere. Unpacking was even more fun than packing because Mama didn't seem the least bit worried about the mess.

"Have you seen or heard anyone?" Kimba asked, hopping up onto the cedar chest next to her sister.

Hiro yawned and stretched out her front legs.

"No," she said, "but Mama and Daddy have been around, so Artemis may just be watching and waiting. He's not going to talk when humans might catch him."

Kimba glanced from her sister to the mirror. Nothing greeted her but their two anxious faces and the inside of the bathroom.

"Kimba," Hiro whispered, "what if the bad guys find us first?"

The fur on Kimba's spine rose, and her ears flushed.

"Artemis won't let that happen. His job is to protect us. Anyway, how could one of those rebels have access to all the computers and stuff that our parents and the special agents use?" Kimba glanced back at the mirror. "No, Artemis will find us first. It has only been a couple of days. Everything will be fine."

Listening from just outside the doorway, Miss Fatty Cat hoped Kimba was wrong. She had spent weeks sharing information and offering assistance wherever she could to the League For Cat Equality. Through her contact with Snowball, the fat cat was prepared to help arrange a kidnapping of either Kimba or Hiro at a moment's notice.

Miss Fatty Cat didn't have any special love for the League's mission to secure the same opportunities for all cats, no matter who their parents were. As an agent of the High Command, the black cat had all the freedom and opportunity any cat could wish for. Her only goal was to see Kimba and Hiro taken down a peg or two. Getting them out of her house for good would be a bonus.

She stalked back into Leia's room and heaved herself onto the bed. This family was supposed to be hers, not one to share with a couple of self-important newbies. The high commander should have transferred her children up to the ship the moment she found them.

Leaving untrained, newly born cats on Earth was against every rule in the book. It was just one of the special treatments that Agent Ebony, Miss Fatty Cat, witnessed every moment she lived with the sisters. Day after day she was forced to listen to the family fuss and coo at Hiro and Kimba. It was revolting.

"Spoiled brats," she grumbled as she curled up for her afternoon nap. "You'll learn the importance of training and rules and protocol when the League gets its paws on you."

Miss Fatty Cat's Revenge

Miss Fatty Cat spent an awful lot of time sleeping, usually on her back.

Chapter 4
BLUE-RIBBON SPECIAL AGENT

Special Agent Medusa Gloriosa heard the voice calling from the living room mirror, and it woke her from her afternoon slumber. Her mummy had just left for work a few minutes ago. Medusa's sleep was disturbed when Mummy kissed the top of her head, but she could forgive her human for waking her to say goodbye. The Cat in the Mirror was not so welcome. He must have been watching and waiting.

"Greetings, Special Agent Medusa. Medusa, can you hear me? We have an urgent situation."

The beautiful Himalayan cat rolled lazily onto her back and stretched all four of her limbs in opposite directions. Maybe he would go away.

"Medusa?" the voice repeated.

"Yes, yes," she mumbled without budging. "I hear you."

There was a moment of silence. Medusa and the Cat in the Mirror waited on each other. The agent cleared his throat.

"Can you please come to the mirror, Special Agent Medusa?"

"Why?" she asked. "What can be so vitally important that you need to interrupt my beauty sleep?"

"There is a mission in your area, and you are the only active agent for miles."

"I am not *active*, Special Agent. I'm retired," she complained, finally rolling over and looking toward the mirror.

"Every trip you have made to Earth has been like a retirement," he said. "Do you remember the last one? You spent twenty years as a pampered show cat."

"A *blue-ribbon champion* show cat, thank you very much. Best in Show four years straight," Medusa corrected, shaking all over so her creamy long fur fell into perfect order.

"Yes, Best in Show. What I'm saying is that it

wasn't a terribly challenging Earth placement for you."

"I can't help being beautiful."

The agent wasn't sure how to respond. They were getting way off track.

"Certainly," he agreed, since this seemed the easiest way to move things along. "But you are also a highly trained agent with two hundred years of experience. I hope you can spare us a few minutes of your retirement years to help us find the daughters of the high commander."

"Felicity's daughters? Well, that's different." Medusa pursed her whiskers. "Why didn't you say it was something so important?"

She leapt down from the red velvet sofa and sauntered over to the middle of the room, where she had a better view of the mirror. The agent waiting for her was not too shabby-looking himself. His long, thick, black-and-white fur was immaculately groomed, and his eyes were bright and alert. Medusa turned her head slightly to the left, showing off her best side.

"I am always happy to help my old friend Felicity. I don't believe we have met, Agent . . ."

"Special Agent Buddy."

"Buddy?" she asked, swishing her amazingly fluffy tail. "That sounds more like an Earth name than an agent one."

"I am keeping the name from my last on-planet assignment. It was an honorable posting with a good family, and it's actually a nickname my brother gave me centuries ago. Sometimes the humans get it right."

"I see," she said, blinking her eyes slowly. She had no intention of keeping her Earth name and being called NumNums once she returned to the ship, no matter how nummy her marvelous mummy thought she was. *Special Agent NumNums? Can you imagine?* she thought. *A cat has got to have some pride.*

Buddy was pretty sure he should be offended, but he didn't have time to argue with the glamorous cat.

"The high commander's two youngest children have been in hiding with an Earth family for over two years. We thought it best to keep them safe from the rebels and their troublemaking."

Medusa squinched her nose, like she had smelled something awful.

"Those rebels are just being ridiculous. Life is much easier when everyone knows their place and stays in it. If Felicity's children are safe on Earth, why all the bother?"

"The children remain hidden, we suspect, but the humans moved unexpectedly, and we lost track of them."

"Hmmm," she said. "Someone must be in big trouble for that one."

"Yes, I'm sure," Buddy said, trying to stay focused. "The human female has been spotted about a mile from your location. She was covered with fresh fur markings from one of the daughters, Kimba. Our hope is that they are still with the family and can be located soon so protection can be restored."

"What do you want from me?"

"The next time your human lets you outside, poke around and see what you can find out. Talk to other cats in the neighborhood and see if any new families have arrived."

Medusa sighed and curled her dark-brown tail daintily around her body.

"I'm sure I can manage it," she said.

"I'm positive you can, Special Agent Medusa Gloriosa," Buddy said.

She held her head high at the sound of her full name, and she purred ever so slightly.

"While we wouldn't cause you the indignity of monitoring your mirror full time, an agent will remain alert to you. Call him if you have any information to share. It is imperative that we find the high commander's children before someone else does."

Medusa bowed her head slightly in response.

What a diva, Buddy thought as he switched off the monitor. As long as she did her job and helped find Kimba and Hiro, he didn't care how many hours a day she spent sleeping on a velvet cushion. He needed whatever help he could get.

Medusa. Quite glorious.

Chapter 5
CRABBY FATTY CAT

Miss Fatty Cat was grateful when the humans left the house. School days gave some sense of order to the humans' comings and goings, but now it was summertime. She had no idea how long they would be gone. Once the sounds of the car on the gravel driveway faded away, she assured herself that Kimba and Hiro were asleep. This house didn't offer the same privacy she had before, but at least there was still a separate bathroom mirror to use.

Plans had been moving forward swimmingly with her contacts in the League For Cat Equality. The move brought total chaos. As long as Snowball could locate their house, the plan could still proceed. If he could beat Artemis to them and have an element of surprise, that was even better.

The round cat leapt up into Leia's bathroom sink. She teetered on the edge, nearly losing her balance. This new bathroom was not as comfortable for communications, but it would have to do.

"Greetings, is anyone there yet?" she whispered.

Still no answer. It would be difficult to sit and wait in the sink all day, and not very comfortable either. Miss Fatty Cat decided the process might speed up if she followed the guidelines for lost agents. It happened now and again on Earth, and every agent knew how to assist the High Command in locating them again.

Dipping her foot in the still-damp sink, she reached up and pressed the pad of her paw on the glass. It left a perfect imprint. Then she wiped the furry back of her foot across the mirror. Now her fur registration would be in plain sight for anyone checking on this particular mirror.

Miss Fatty Cat would have preferred to deal directly with Snowball, but he had been silent for too long. She didn't want to end her life stuck here on

Earth. It was best to help the agents on the ship to locate them all right away. If Snowball didn't find them first, the League would have to start planning again, but found was better than lost, either way.

She callumped onto the ground and curled up on a rug in the middle of the bathroom. If Snowball checked this mirror, she would be ready and waiting.

This was not what Agent Ebony had imagined for her second visit to Earth. She was a trained agent and had been looking forward to working her way up in the ranks. The High Council had even allowed her timid sister to come with her in the hopes of toughening her up a bit. They could never have anticipated that Agent Onyx would squander her Earth time by cuddling with a human or hiding under a bed.

What a waste, Ebony (Miss Fatty Cat) thought.

Every step of their placement with the pet rescue group and their adoption by the family had been carefully monitored. If it had been a bad placement, both black cats would have been returned to the ship immediately. The home appeared to be safe and loving, so they settled in.

Agent Ebony was now named Miss Fatty Cat by her human. That was fairly disgraceful, but there were worse names. As ordered by the High Command, she made contact with headquarters through Leia's bathroom mirror. Her only mission at the time was to experience Earth life and report back. Being a little girl's plaything was not part of the deal. Slinky had been paired up with the older daughter, Mindy. Miss Fatty Cat had become Leia's cherished possession.

Fatty Cat had been dressed up in lacy clothes. She had been pushed around in a stroller and forced to watch hours of mind-numbing television. She had been clutched and brushed and trapped in the bedroom. None of this would be of any use to the High Council. That fact was becoming crystal clear. She could see the smirk on Regalus's face every time she admitted to an honest report about her days on Earth.

Soon she had refused to report anything. It was too shameful. She had broken off all communication with the Cats in the Mirror. Fatty never planned on speaking to them again until her Earth mission was complete and she could finally return to the ship.

When the new kittens arrived, it became increasingly difficult to avoid. The first time Miss Fatty Cat had snuck into the grown-ups' bathroom to sneak a peek at them, Regalus had been waiting.

"Your mission has taken a turn for the better," he had insisted. "These kittens are of vital importance to the high commander and require special care and attention."

They hadn't seemed very special to her. Why should some stupid little kittens who didn't even understand their alien heritage be more important than an agent like her? She had turned her back on Regalus and refused to help. When Kimba had asked her about it, she even denied knowing anything about the Cats in the Mirror. She was done with all of them.

Then Snowball found her. She had been minding her own business, getting a drink from Leia's sink, when the fluffy, flat-faced white cat with the bright-green eyes appeared in the bathroom mirror.

At first, Snowball had pretended to be a normal agent, trying to win Miss Fatty Cat back to making reports again. But once he realized how truly angry and resentful the black cat had become, he told her about who Kimba and Hiro were and about the League For Cat Equality.

"Our only goal is for all cats to have the same

opportunities," he had explained. "Every cat should be able to grow up to be an agent or to be on the High Council. If he has the right talents and abilities, he might even become a commander. Cats who are born to be workers never have a chance to visit Earth. Those cats have endured enough injustice. We want the freedom that every cat naturally desires."

It hadn't taken him many days to get to the point. The League For Cat Equality knew all about the high commander's two young daughters hiding in Miss Fatty Cat's house. Getting their paws on Kimba and Hiro would be the perfect bargaining tool to force the High Council to accept their demands.

All Miss Fatty Cat had to do was to help out and share what she heard and saw. One day, when the timing was perfect, she could help them to locate the sisters directly and assist in an unauthorized transfer.

In the beginning, Miss Fatty Cat had refused to help. She didn't want to be banished on Earth. She liked the special privileges of being an agent. She had no intention of messing up the order of her cat life once she returned to the ship. But as the days wore on, she watched Kimba and Hiro become more and more pampered. Jealousy got the best of her.

While she was forced to sleep all night with Leia, Kimba was given total freedom. The white cat even had special beds all over the house for her use only. While Miss Fatty Cat was forced to have tea parties with Leia, Hiro was given her own private food bowl and special human cheese crackers whenever she wanted. Day after day, it rubbed the fat cat's fur the wrong way.

Then one night the royal sisters got an actual birthday party with cake and presents and everything. Miss Fatty Cat had had enough. Giving them a good thawumping now and then no longer made her feel better. She wanted revenge. That very day she offered up her services to Snowball, the transfer operations specialist.

The fat cat really had no interest in equality for all cats. She didn't care about the goals of the League For Cat Equality. As a well-born agent, every door on the spaceship was open to her. Mostly, she wanted justice. To her that meant seeing Kimba and Hiro get a taste of how other cats live. Maybe they should even suffer a little bit. This was only their first life, and they needed to learn some harsh realities.

If Snowball wants to catch them and scare them and hold them hostage, more power to him.

The house move had created a bit of a delay, but Miss Fatty Cat was certain the family would be found eventually. Then everything could proceed as planned. She settled down on the rug to wait for the agent who would surely notice her marks on the mirror and find them all.

Chapter 6
AN UNAUTHORIZED TRANSFER

"Specialist Snowball," an orange tabby cat called from across the room. "Come look at this!"

Snowball had been dozing at his computer monitor, desperately trying to avoid going off duty and missing his moment to strike. His head lurched up, and he glared at the agent. Then he realized there could only be one reason for the interruption. The tabby had found the sisters.

Trying to appear calm, Snowball trotted across the control room and stood on his back legs so he could see the tabby's computer screen. All he saw was a photo of the Eiffel Tower on the back wall of a purple bathroom.

"Why did you bother me?" he growled. "There's nothing there."

"Look closer. Look at the glass," the agent grumbled, annoyed by the rude transfer technician who shouldn't even be in a room full of skilled agents.

Snowball focused on the bottom of the glass, and this time he noticed the paw print and fur smear. Tapping out some keys on the computer, he had his answer. The fur registered to Agent Ebony, and the paw print was a match.

"Good catch, Agent," Snowball said.

The tabby flicked his whiskers. There was no way he would have missed such an obvious marking. It was part of any decent agent's training.

"We should report it to Special Agent Artemis immediately."

"Of course, of course, I will do that," Snowball said quickly, and he dashed for his computer.

"I should report it, Specialist Snowball," the tabby called after him.

Snowball froze in his tracks. Protocol dictated that the agent should tell Artemis himself. Under normal circumstances they would never communicate through a transfer technician. Snowball was grateful that his decades of work with the High

Command had put him in a trusted position today. He needed to reach the sisters first.

"No, no, that's fine," he said, trying to sound casual. "I already assured Artemis that I would contact him myself the moment I heard anything. Remember, he said that anyone who found a sign of the sisters should let me know. I will tell him. See what else you can find out about the location of that mirror."

He hoped to keep the agent busy for a few minutes. The tabby was annoyed at Snowball's upstart behavior, but he did as he was told. At least the high commander's daughters had been found. They must be in the same house, he decided. After the longest shift of his life, the tabby was happy to be done with this assignment. He was too tired to worry about who told Artemis.

Snowball hopped up into his computer chair, but he did not contact Artemis. Tapping in the location he had seen on the tabby's monitor, Snowball pulled up the mirror in Agent Ebony's location. He couldn't risk appearing in the mirror, but he could hear deep snoring noises from somewhere in the room. Snowball opened a voice-only communication window.

"Greetings, Agent Ebony," he whispered. "Are you there?"

There was a startled snort. Miss Fatty Cat had fallen asleep on the bathmat and was grateful she was out of view of the mirror. She stretched, waggling her large bottom in the air. Listening at the door for a moment, she confirmed that the family had not returned. Then she jumped up onto the sink ledge and stared into the mirror.

"This is Agent Ebony," she whispered back. "Who's there? It's okay. The humans are not home."

Snowball opened a full communications window, and Miss Fatty Cat sighed in relief.

"You noticed my markings on the mirror?" she asked.

"Yes, that's how we found you. Are Kimba and Hiro and your sister at this location as well?"

"Yes," she continued in a whisper. "But this mirror is in a separate room."

"Good," Snowball said, hesitantly looking around the control room.

No one was paying any attention to him. Word had spread that the sisters' home had been found, and everyone was grateful and taking a break or heading to the dining hall. In a few minutes, he would be the only one left in his sector. A side portion of his screen lit up, showing maps and lists of information.

"I sent you the local scan," the tabby said as he wandered by. "That should be everything you need to help get them set up at the new location."

Snowball's eyes narrowed, worried that the tabby had noticed Agent Ebony on the screen as well. Seeing them talking might make him suspicious, but he walked past the monitor without even glancing in that direction. All of the agents on duty were hungry and ready for naps. This gave the League the moment they had been waiting for. There was no time for a meeting. Snowball knew he needed to act alone and act fast. He leaned in close to the monitor.

"Agent Ebony, do you know where Kimba is right now?"

"I'm not sure." The fat cat tilted her head to one side. "She was asleep downstairs a while ago."

"Go and locate her, quickly," Snowball whispered. "The plan is going into operation now."

"Right now?" she asked.

"Yes. I will figure it all out while you find the white one. Whatever you do, don't wake her. We can only make the surprise transfer safely if she is asleep."

Eyes wide, Miss Fatty Cat thumped down from the sink and began searching the house. Kimba was not on the dining room chair or the sofa, so she headed downstairs.

Back at headquarters, Snowball enlarged the local information on the screen. He needed somewhere to hide Kimba, and he needed it immediately while they had the element of surprise. Then the League could prove they were really serious.

The League had never given Snowball definite plans about how the kidnapping would happen, so he needed to make his own decision. A large chunk of land near Kimba's location caught his eye. There were Xs and names covering vast portions of it. It appeared to be a zoo.

Headquarters tried to keep track of every big cat in every zoo in the world, even if they never made contact. Did this zoo only have big cats? Focusing in closer, Snowball saw photo displays for tigers and lions and cougars and panthers.

Perfect, he thought.

Snowball rapidly jotted down the specific coordinates and then reduced the screen again. He opened the file on the house just as the fat cat lumbered into the bathroom and heaved herself into the sink again.

"She is asleep . . . on the sofa . . . downstairs . . . in the game room," Miss Fatty Cat reported, huffing and puffing after her climb up the stairs.

Snowball scanned and typed and adjusted the numbers on the screen until he had a lock on Kimba's fur registration. It was a process used to retrieve agents in desperate situations or from a vet's office at the end of their Earth-life. As long as the general location was known, the scans worked effectively. Snowball had seen it done and had learned well.

Looking around the nearly empty room again, Snowball sent both sets of coordinates to the transfer controls. The last part would be the easiest for him. Transferring an agent was a tricky job, but he was a specialist. He even knew how to hide this unauthorized transfer so no one would ever notice it.

"Thank you, Agent Ebony," he said, blinking his eyes slowly. "That is all we need from you for now, but be alert. Hiro will be next."

Snowball closed the communication window before she could reply. The transfer needed to be done, and he would have to report to Artemis before another agent got wise to him. Working his way nonchalantly across the room, Snowball climbed onto the transfer platform. He wandered around the controls, as if he were checking for some lost notes or something else unimportant.

When he was positive no one was paying attention, he completed the transfer process and returned to his computer. Snowball couldn't believe how easy it had been and how impressed the League would be by his remarkable plan. He imagined the praise and congratulations he'd receive from every cat in the League when they heard about the kidnapping he had pulled off single-handedly. His tail thrashed with pride at his noble accomplishment.

KIMBA'S NAP was disturbed by a strange tingling sensation. It was vaguely familiar, but in the fog of sleep, she couldn't place it. There was a bright light. Then the sensation stopped. The air around her smelled odd. Birds were chirping and the wind blew past her, ruffling her coat. Kimba's head snapped up, fur puffed and ears on full alert.

Kimba was no longer on the sofa in the girls' game room downstairs in their new house. She was outside. The blue sky loomed large above her, and the summer sun beat down on her white head with a blinding brilliance. She could feel soft grass under her paws.

As her sensitive eyes adjusted, she noticed a tall metal fence reaching up into the sky. There were dozens of strange odors she couldn't identify. This was nothing like home.

Where in the world am I, and how did I get here? she wondered in a panic. She remembered the tingling and the bright light. *Someone used the transfer machine on me*, she realized in horror.

The rebels must have found them first. Just like that, she had been picked up from her safe home and placed who knows where. She was lost.

A low rumbling noise came from behind her. It was unlike anything she had ever heard before, and it vibrated through her bones and out the tips of her whiskers. Slowly, Kimba turned to face whatever had made that horrible sound.

It was worse than her nightmares.

Chapter 7
KARMA

Kimba hunkered in the grass, horrified. Lying just a few feet away was an enormous, gargantuan cat. Her tawny fur had light-brown stripes running through it, but her face was covered with black dots. The dots formed a beautiful design that seemed to be painted in perfect order. Kimba was in awe of the creature's beauty and terrified to her core at the same time. She was the same size as one of those paws!

The two cats locked eyes, but Kimba quickly looked down. The striped cat rumbled again, and Kimba struggled not to hiss or run.

Show respect, she coached herself. *Be still and don't freak out. Maybe she won't eat you in one bite.*

"You arrived very suddenly, little one," the huge cat said.

Kimba swallowed hard, keeping her eyes focused on the grass beneath her feet.

"Yes, I did. I'm sorry about that. I didn't mean to invade your territory," Kimba whispered humbly.

"Hmmm," the big cat rumbled. "Do you intend on staying?"

"No, ma'am. I need to find a way to get back to my home. I promise not to bother you at all if you can just show me how to get out of the fence."

"You are not a bother," she said. "Having you appear in my enclosure is one of the most exciting things that has happened in many weeks."

Kimba glanced up tentatively and met the cat's eyes again. They were perfectly golden and surrounded by a ring of white fur. The creature didn't seem angry, so Kimba relaxed a tiny bit and her fur lowered.

"What is your name, white, stripe-less one?"

"My name is Kimba, ma'am. I'm named after a famous white lion, but I'm only a house cat."

"I have never met a house cat before," she said. "You look rather like a baby white tiger with no stripes. It is nice to meet you, Kimba. I am Karma."

"That's a lovely name," Kimba said, minding her manners. Paying Karma a compliment seemed to be a good idea. "You're very beautiful. I've never heard of a lion with stripes and spots before."

The huge cat rumbled deep in her chest with pride.

"I am not a lion. I am a liger."

"A *liger*?" Kimba asked. "Mama watches a lot of nature TV shows, but I've never seen or heard of a liger before."

"During guest tours, the keepers say that a liger is an unnatural mixed breed created by humans because we look interesting and beautiful. My father was a lion, and my mother was a tiger. Those two cats do not even live on the same continent, but humans enjoy messing around with things like that."

"Amazing."

"The biggest problem the humans find with our breed is that we never really stop growing. The keepers say that one liger grew to be almost a thousand pounds. Ligers can be supersized, so we are a very impressive group."

Kimba nodded slowly in total agreement. *Impressive, to say the least.*

Kimba wanted to ask about a hundred other

questions, but she was grateful to still be alive in the presence of this beast. She decided not to push her luck.

She looked around the fenced-in area, hoping for an easy escape. No cat wants to overstay her welcome. Karma would get hungry eventually, but what was on the other side of the fence could be even worse. The liger studied Kimba's eyes and sensed her confusion.

"Do you understand where you are, little Kimba?"

"No." Kimba sat up and sighed deeply. "Not even a little bit."

"You are with Karma the liger in her enclosure at Turpentine Creek Wildlife Refuge in Arkansas."

At least I'm still in Arkansas, she thought. But knowing where she was didn't really solve the problem of how to get home.

"What's on the other side of the fence?" Kimba asked.

"From what I have seen from my homes in various places around the refuge, there are dozens and dozens of lions and tigers and cougars and other cats living in fenced areas just like mine. Some have grass. Some are smaller. The humans keep building more enclosures, but more rescued cats arrive all the time. I am lucky to have such a large area."

Kimba's fur rose on her back again at the thought of being surrounded by that many big cats. She would have to avoid them at all costs. This one seemed very nice, but there was no way to tell about the others. A tiny house cat would be nothing more than a play toy to them. She glanced back at Karma's massive paws. She needed to find her way out of this liger's yard, and soon.

"Is there a way for me to get out of the fence?" she asked.

"Well, you don't want to go that way." Karma nodded to the left. "There are tigers in that section."

Kimba couldn't see any tigers past the fence line on that side, but she would take Karma's word for it.

"But if you go out behind you, it will lead you to open space and the road the humans use to travel around the refuge. I believe you are small enough to walk right through the first fence without any trouble."

Kimba hadn't considered that option. All she saw were walls blocking her freedom. She rose cautiously and slunk over to the fence. It was true. The gaps in the fence were large enough for a house cat to slip out.

"You're right, Karma. I can fit."

"Then you should probably do that soon."

From her position near the fence, Kimba noticed something she hadn't seen before. They were not alone. In the far corner of the enclosure, another liger, even bigger than Karma, was sleeping on his back. His massive striped legs were up in the air, leaning on the fence. He was happily snoring.

Karma blinked slowly and swished her tail.

"That is my brother, Brady. He is very fussy about his territory."

Hearing his name, the male liger snorted, rolled onto his side, and lifted his head groggily. His short mane was rumpled, but he was very impressive.

Without a second thought, Kimba skittered through the fencing to safety on the other side. Karma chuffed at her brother, and he plopped his head back down to sleep.

Kimba was now free from the liger enclosure, but there was another fence between her and the dirt road. Those bars were closer together. Squeezing through was not an option, and the fence ran along the entire length of the big cat yards as far as she could see.

"Can you climb, little Kimba?" the liger called to her.

Kimba's eyes trailed up the wall of fencing to the top far above her. It was taller than Daddy, but not much taller than the ladders at home. Kimba loved to climb ladders.

"I can climb, but I've never gone this straight up."

"There may be another way out of that fence, but I doubt it. Safety is very important around here."

Kimba noticed a thick-maned male lion watching her from a yard across the road. Normally she was not a big fan of fences, but today she was grateful for them. In this narrow area between barriers, she was safe from the tigers and lions, but she was not free and not any closer to getting home.

One glance at the sky told Kimba that it would be getting dark soon. She had only been outside one other time in her life. It had been horrible, but that time at least she knew where her home and family were. She had gotten back inside before dark. Now she was all alone, and the sun was setting.

"There are many creatures living in the woods

around here who are not contained by fences, little Kimba," Karma called to her. "Hunting hawks and eagles can reach you where you are, even if others could not. I would advise that you seek help from the humans before dark. Follow the road up the hill over there, and you will surely find them. That's the direction where the humans walk, but the last group has already gone by today. Even if you can't find the humans themselves, you will be safer if you can hide closer to where the keepers are. Wild things don't go near the humans."

"Thank you, Karma. You've been very kind," she said, eyeing the sky for any large hungry birds. Then an interesting thought crossed her mind. "You know, I think I was put in your yard on purpose. The cats who did it don't like me much. I think they hoped you would eat me."

"Hmmm," the liger pondered. "Brady might have attacked you, but you wouldn't make a very good meal. Too tiny."

Kimba had never been so happy to be small.

"They may send my sister here as well. She looks like me, but she is black and white. She will be very, very scared. Can you please direct her toward the humans too."

"Of course, Kimba. I will do my best to help you find each other."

"Thank you, Karma. Goodbye."

The liger blinked slowly in return and watched with interest as Kimba crept her way along the fence, staying low to the ground.

"Good luck, tiny white lion," Karma called softly in return.

Kimba loved to climb ladders. If one came out, she was up to the top immediately.

Miss Fatty Cat's Revenge

Karma liger in the snow at Turpentine Creek Wildlife Refuge.

Brady liger on his bench at Turpentine Creek Wildlife Refuge.

Chapter 8
HORUS IS UNIMPRESSED

After notifying Artemis about the location of Miss Fatty Cat and the family, Snowball headed back to his private quarters on a lower deck of the ship. It was unusual for a cat of his status to live alone. Most had to share.

For over one hundred years of service, Snowball had worked his way up through the ranks. His long and valuable assistance to the High Command earned him special privileges that came in handy for his work with the rebel group. That was certainly not what Felicity had in mind when she arranged for the honor of a private room.

Settling in on a cushion, Snowball opened a private communication window with Horus, the leader of the League For Cat Equality. The stern, glum face of a longhaired black cat stared at him. Her deep-yellow eyes glowed in the darkness of the secret meeting room.

"Have you found them?" she asked.

"Yes, Commander Horus. Agent Ebony was actually located first, so there was a prime opportunity to grab Kimba before the high commander even knew they had been found."

The black cat shifted uncomfortably.

"You have already taken action?"

"Yes. I didn't want to lose our chance to act before the High Council got involved again. Kimba was successfully transferred into the cage of a big cat not far from her home."

"Are you saying that Kimba has been assassinated? That she is dead?" The black cat's yellow eyes narrowed, and her whiskers tensed in anger.

Snowball was expecting praise for his quick thinking and bold actions. He swallowed hard.

"I don't have proof of what happened to her, Commander. I just know that she was transferred into the cage. She probably made it out okay."

"The plan was to capture the sisters and use

them as a bargaining tool. Was I not clear on that? A dead cat is of no use to us."

Snowball felt a lump like a huge fur ball settle in his throat.

"But now the high commander will know that we are serious. When we grab Hiro, she will know what we are capable of. She will have to listen to our demands."

"Clearly, that will have to be the way we proceed," the rebel leader mumbled. "Do you have a location for the second daughter from that litter? It won't be long before they notice Kimba is missing and give extra protection to the other one."

"Yes, Commander," Snowball said, "but I'm sure Artemis has already found her through another mirror at that location. I had to tell him about finding Agent Ebony and the house. Everyone in the control room knew about it. Artemis would have become suspicious of me if I didn't report it. It will be tricky to get Hiro out now, but it can be done."

"Very well. When you see your chance, transfer her out. Here are the coordinates of a hidden room in the ship where you can send Hiro. No one will look for her there. We need her tucked away and alive. Do exactly as you are told this time. No more random lion cages, Specialist Snowball. Do you understand?"

Snowball studied the maps that Horus sent.

"I know right where that is," he said. "My ancestors have been responsible for the maintenance and care of this ship for thousands of years. Having family who have to clean every nook and cranny of a spaceship has its advantages. Well, not many advantages, but this time it's helpful. I know my way around areas no agent would ever think to look."

"Good. We need to be quick. Watch for your opportunity, and keep me informed once Hiro is in our hands. You need to find Kimba and transfer her to the holding room as well. If she is not alive, it could get complicated. Find her. Move her. We need them both alive and unharmed. Do you understand what you need to do, Snowball?"

"Yes, Commander. Absolutely," he said.

"Good. Get it done now."

With that, Horus vanished from the monitor. Snowball sighed and crouched down on the pillow. He hadn't thought much past kidnapping and getting rid of Kimba, and he had no idea how he was going to find her again.

Chapter 9
LIONS AND TIGERS AND BEARS

Kimba crept along the road at the refuge, being sure to stay hidden in the grass and along the fence line as much as possible. On either side of her, the smell of more lions and tigers and the strong odor of fresh raw meat was overpowering.

Thankfully, Karma had already been fed. That was a lucky break. Otherwise, she might not have been so friendly. The thought of it sent a shiver up Kimba's spine, and her tail puffed.

That must have been the rebel's plan for me. Liger chow. She had survived that much, at least.

When she reached the end of the fence where the road started a dramatic upward slope, she could see that Karma was right. The bars in this area attached to the other line of fencing, and she was trapped. Crouching low and looking up the hill, Kimba noticed a gigantic enclosure up ahead. Beyond that, there were several large buildings.

Those must be where the humans are, she thought.

Kimba had never met a human who didn't adore her. They all thought she was amazing. She hoped whatever humans she found in this strange place were the same. It was certainly a better idea than a night outside and alone. She would have to climb the fence and hope for the best.

Testing the first steps on the wire fencing, she discovered that it was rough on her soft, indoor paw pads, but it was strong. If she moved quickly, pulling with her whole paw wrapped around each bar, she could reach the top. That was how she climbed Daddy's ladders at home. The same strategy should work here. The top of the fence was flat, not curved inward like the fence on the enclosures. Once she got to the top, she would simply jump to the ground below.

Or fall, she worried.

Taking several deep breaths, Kimba placed her front paws on the fence and waggled her bottom in preparation. Her still-puffy white tail thrashed, ready to help her balance as she climbed. With a last gasp, Kimba pulled with her front legs and hopped her back feet onto the fence. Then, one paw at a time, she dragged her body along the bars. The fence dug into her legs with sharp stabs of pain, but she kept moving.

Reaching the top, she pulled her upper half over and found herself draped across the fence. She balanced there for a minute with the top bar jabbing into her belly, then she began to slip. With a mighty push from her back legs, Kimba flew over the top of the fence.

Her legs flailed wildly in the air for a split second as she tumbled, but she leveled out quickly. Millions of years of feline instinct pulled her feet into place, and she landed with a thunk on the grass next to the road. The ground was covered with rocks that cut at her paws, but sore feet were a small sacrifice for freedom. Clear of the fence now, she prepared to face whatever lay ahead.

Testing the air, Kimba couldn't detect any human odors. The pungent smells of meat and poop and dozens of big cats overwhelmed everything else. Aiming her nose at the large enclosure up ahead,

Kimba sensed something different. It was definitely not a cat.

Staying low to the ground, she crept up the steep sidewalk that led past the vast fenced-in area and toward the human buildings. Another fence blocked her way to this part of the refuge, but it was only designed to keep people out. She easily wiggled under the gate.

Kimba slunk up the sidewalk past an enclosure that was three times the size of Karma's. Inside the fence, she saw an enormous, brown, furry creature. He was snuffling his way along the edges of his home with his giant muzzle pressed against the ground. Every time he came across weeds growing within reach, he snorted and grumbled and gobbled them up.

Standing on the sidewalk across from the creature, Kimba saw his long, impressive claws. They were horrifying and as thick as her tail. Her eyes trailed up the massive leg to the even more massive body and finally to the gargantuan head of a monster.

He looked like The Big Black Beast, not a cat. This animal's ears were round instead of pointy, and his snout was long with a leathery black nose at the end.

The snuffling noises coming from it made her fur rise and brought back those outdoor feelings of wanting to run and hide and climb. Her nose and ears flushed pink, but she held her ground.

Whatever that is, there are metal bars between us.

Taking a break from his foraging, he noticed her watching him. The creature tipped his head to one side and flapped his lips as he sniffed in her direction. She saw his huge fangs hiding in his long snout.

Oh my! Kimba gulped.

"You iz the smallest cat I haz ever seen," he said in a deep, rumbly voice.

Despite his appearance, he seemed to be friendly. It reminded her of the first time she had talked to The Big Black Beast. Miss Fatty Cat had made him sound so scary. The Beast had turned out to be nothing more than a goofball, but this creature's claws were as impressive as a saber-tooth cat's fangs. She kept her distance from the fence and sat down on the sidewalk.

"I would imagine I seem small to you," Kimba managed to answer in her most polite voice.

"And you don't look likez the other kittiez here," he continued. "There are white onez, but they are stripey. Everyone else iz brownish or spotted or black or something else like that. You iz a super-tiny-white-little kitty. My foot iz bigger than you," he said, stretching it out toward her. He seemed very amused by this idea.

"My name is Kimba," she said. "And I'm afraid I'm a bit lost."

"Oooh," he sighed. "I'm not. Thiz iz my home."

"That's good," she said. "Lost is not a happy feeling."

"When I waz a tiny baby, I used to live in a barn in an eensy-weensy cage. That wasn't a happy feeling either."

He lowered his head in sadness at the memory.

"That doesn't sound very happy," Kimba agreed.

"But now I livez here." He perked up. The creature sat back on his round bottom and stuck his leathery back feet out in front of him. Grabbing his clawed toes with his front feet, he rocked back and forth with the rhythm of his words. "And I haz a climby house . . . and a swimmy pool . . . and people come by to see me . . . all day long . . . and take picturez of me . . . and they laugh . . . when I am silly. I haz lotz of friendz now."

"That sounds great," Kimba agreed.

A memory of Mama floated across her mind—

playing string with her and laughing and taking pictures. *Mama*. Would she ever see her again? She shook her head to clear the worried thoughts and focus on the animal here and now. Maybe he could help her.

"I don't want to sound rude," she continued, "but what are you? I've never seen anything quite like you before either."

"Iz a grizzzzzzly bear," he chortled with glee. "Roooowrrrr!" He fake-snarled, showing off an impressive set of teeth and fangs. "But I'z still only five. The keeperz sayz I'm gonna get bigger and bigger and bigger. Roooowrrrr!" The bear rocked back with the force of his growl.

Kimba didn't know exactly what a grizzly bear was, but he would be scary to meet if the fence wasn't there. She would ask one of the Cats in the Mirror about bears when she got home. If she got home. Her ears lowered at the thought of it.

"Bam Bam!" a human voice called from the other side of the enclosure.

The bear turned his massive head to look and almost tipped over backward. Then he leaned back toward Kimba.

"It'z time for me to go to bed," he said, a tinge of sadness in his voice.

"The humans tell you when to go to bed?" she marveled. Convincing the massive grizzly bear to do anything seemed like a dangerous job.

"We haz to go inside our housez at darknezz time," Bam Bam said. "The keeperz say it'z safer that way. Only the onez up at the front of the refuge on the hard floorz get to stay out at night. They don't have any grazz or yardz or anything yet. I used to have a cage up there and got to stay out at night. I'd rather have my big new yard and all my toyz and my pool and my climby thing and get locked up at night."

Kimba heard clanging noises as huge doors opened in a building at the far end of the fencing. The monstrous bear flopped onto his back, scratching it on the rough ground, all four paws flailing around in the air. Then he sighed and clamored to his feet, shaking off the excess dust.

"I haz to go now," he said to Kimba. "Will you be herez tomorrow?"

"I'm not sure," she admitted. "But I need to find a safe place to spend the night."

"You could try to sneak into my house with me,"

he said, a forlorn note in his deep voice. "It'z really big, and there iz hay to sleep in and chicken and berriez and nutz to munch on."

Kimba pictured the massive fangs she had seen a moment ago and thought she had better pass. He seemed good-natured enough, but if he ate chicken, he might just eat house cats too.

"Thank you so much. I may come back this way if I can't find a human to help me."

That wasn't totally a lie. Hiding out in his fenced area was a better option than the mountain forest around the refuge.

"Okie dokie," he said. "Well, nighty-nightz then. And good luck not being lost anymore."

He waddled his way over to the giant doorway and lumbered inside. On the far side of the building, Kimba saw a human in a tan outfit pushing the door closed from outside the fence. Then there was a huge clunking sound, just like the deadbolt on the front door at home. Bam Bam was locked in for the night.

The human walked farther up the hillside, so Kimba followed in that direction as well. There were several fences between them, but maybe she could find another human. Echoes of other doors closing cats and bears inside for the night rang through the mountains around her.

I'd better find a place for the night soon too, she thought. *If they lock up lions and tigers and bears, what hope do I have?*

Bam Bam the grizzly bear in his swimming pool at Turpentine Creek Wildlife Refuge.

Chapter 10
WHAT SLINKY SAW

The light coming in the windows had faded, and Hiro lazily roused from her evening nap. She could hear the echoed, happy sound of dinner dishes clinking in the kitchen sink. Next the family would gather for some television time before bed. The tuxedo cat enjoyed that time of day, listening to the family laugh and talk together.

Sliding down from her pillow, she headed into the bathroom for a quick snack before joining them. Kimba could take a turn sleeping in front of the mirror.

Hiro wondered if their space-traveling parents had found them yet. There was no way to know for sure. With the human family in the next room, it was too dangerous to try to communicate, so she headed out to join them.

Kimba was normally around in the evenings as well. She enjoyed hanging out in the bathroom with Leia while the girl got ready for bed. It was a great time to get drinks from the bathtub faucet. As the family settled in, Hiro wandered around the living room to pick the best spot for this evening. Kimba usually selected her old favorite dining room chair, but tonight she was nowhere to be seen.

That's weird, Hiro thought. *Kimba loves evening time as much as me.*

She wondered what Kimba was up to and why she hadn't shown up to take a shift in front of the mirror as they had planned. Maybe she had seen something in another house mirror. Hiro searched in Leia's bathroom. No Kimba. She searched in Mama's office downstairs. No Kimba.

"Hello?" Hiro called through the basement rooms. "Kimba?"

She heard Slinky skitter around in Mindy's bedroom and headed in that direction. Peeking through the doorway, Hiro could just see the glow of Slinky's eyes under the bed in the dark. Their paths didn't cross very often. Talking to the skinny black cat was rare, but maybe she knew something about where Kimba was. Hiro was starting to get worried. Any little clue might help.

"Slinky, have you seen Kimba tonight?" Hiro whispered into the bedroom.

"Eeep," was all she heard from under the bed.

Man, she's afraid of everything, Hiro thought, but she tried again.

"I can't find Kimba. Have you seen her?"

The glowing yellow eyes crept closer to the edge of the bed, and Hiro could almost make out the shape of the skittery cat's face.

"The light took her away," Slinky squeaked.

"What light?" Hiro asked, a sinking feeling in the pit of her stomach.

"She was sleeping up on the back of the sofa, right next to where you are now. I could see her from the bedroom. Then I felt something creepy and weird in the air. It made my fur tingle. When I looked up, there was a really bright light all around her."

"Then what?" Hiro insisted.

"Then she was gone," Slinky whispered in horror.

"Gone?"

"Gone," Slinky squeaked.

Gone. Hiro knew what the light meant. Someone

had transferred Kimba. If she had returned since then, she would certainly have found Hiro to let her know what had happened. She was gone.

"Do you know where she went?" Slinky asked.

"No," Hiro admitted, "but I have to find out."

The black-and-white cat raced up the basement stairs, through the house, right past the family in the living room, slipped and slid around the corner, and ran into Mama and Daddy's bedroom.

"What's up with Hiro?" Mama laughed.

"Who knows?" Daddy said, and they all went back to watching the TV.

Hiro leapt onto the bathroom counter and hoped that a Cat in the Mirror had found them and was watching.

"Hello? Artemis? Anyone?" She gasped for air, but continued. "I know you won't show yourselves with the family in the house, but Kimba is gone. Earlier today, Slinky saw someone transfer her out of the house. Someone took her when she was asleep. I can't imagine it was any of you, so that can only mean that the rebels have Kimba. I repeat: The rebels have Kimba!"

Hiro sucked in one more gasp of air and hunkered down on the counter. That was all she could do for now. Her only hope was that someone heard her and would know what to do.

Her tummy clenched and knotted. She had not been this worried since the family went away and left them all alone for a week, but then she had known they were safe. Now, she was pretty sure that Kimba was NOT safe.

Maybe she was urgently needed on the ship, and they didn't have time to warn her, Hiro hoped. *Maybe it's all just a big misunderstanding.*

Daddy came into the bathroom and interrupted her thoughts.

"What are you hollering about in here?" He laughed. "Come on and join us in the living room, silly baby."

He scooped her up and carried her over his shoulder into the other room. Hiro crouched hesitantly on the arm of the sofa. TV time was not the same when her sister was in danger, and she was going to have to sneak back in to wait in front of the mirror again. It was going to be a long night.

Her sister. Her only sister. Kimba was gone.

Slinky did come out from under the bed sometimes. She loved the old, worn sofas in Mama's office, where it was quiet.

Chapter 11
TRACING THE TRANSFER

Hiro got lucky. An agent was watching through the mirror. Once the discovery of Miss Fatty Cat's paw print was reported, it had only taken Artemis a few minutes to search the house and see Hiro sleeping in plain view of the bathroom mirror. The sisters had been found. He notified their mother, the high commander, immediately.

"Oh, thank goodness," Felicity had sighed. "The only reason I allowed them to stay on Earth was so we could monitor them carefully and keep them hidden. Wait for your chance to make contact, and alert me if there is any new information. I'll be in a meeting of the High Council for several hours."

Now, Special Agent Artemis stared at the mirror

in shock as he watched Hiro being carried from the bathroom by the human male. He didn't dare respond to her cries for help, but he had heard her loud and clear.

The rebels have Kimba? It didn't make any sense. Headquarters had just discovered the location of the sisters. It had barely been an hour or two. *How could the League For Cat Equality have found her first?*

He knew he would have to tell their mother right away, and he knew she would be heartbroken and furious. What demands would the rebels make for Kimba's release? His brain spun with uncertainties. Artemis knew it would help him break the news to the high commander if he already had a plan in place.

The first step was easy. All transfers to and from and around Earth must be stopped immediately. Hiro may not have realized that she was also in danger, but Artemis was sure of it. The rebels could not be allowed to capture her, no matter how many others were inconvenienced.

No agents would leave the ship, and none of them would be transferred anywhere without the high commander's permission. He could blame it on a temporary problem with the system. Artemis sent out the order and watched as the transfer machine in his sector was turned off.

Good. That will keep Hiro safe for now. However, it would certainly anger a lot of agents to have their scheduled transfers delayed. Only the fear of a problem with the system would keep them quiet. Every agent had heard stories about a transfer gone wrong. No cat would want to risk it, but they would get antsy. The Command Team was going to have to move fast.

Next, he would have to find Kimba. If he could at least tell the high commander where her daughter was and that she was okay, it would soften the news some.

Is there a way to locate that transfer and discover where she was sent? Artemis wondered. He had studied the transfer system during his training as an agent, but that was decades ago. He couldn't even remember an unauthorized transfer happening within his lifetime. Could it be traced? With a few taps of his keyboard, Artemis contacted the transfer operator on duty in his control room.

"Yes, sir, Special Agent Artemis?" a skinny young tortoiseshell cat answered officially.

He appeared new to the job and a bit terrified,

but Artemis hoped his fresh training would come in handy.

"Is there a way to trace a transfer that happened today?"

"A way to *trace it*, sir? The history of all transfers is available right here in the system records."

"If an *unauthorized* transfer were made on Earth, one that was not officially recorded, can you look back and see exactly what was done?"

The tortie's eyes widened, and his ears lowered.

"Any transfer can be traced, sir, if you have enough time and information. But an unauthorized transfer? Why would someone conduct unauthorized transfers?"

Artemis hesitated, not sure how much he could trust this young cat or how much he should reveal. The blacks of the tortie's eyes spread, and his ears flattened.

"Is this about the high commander's missing children? Has something horrible happened? I thought they had been found."

"Yes," Artemis admitted. "It has to do with that situation. Can you help, Transfer Specialist...?"

"Thoth, sir. My name is Thoth. But I'm just a trainee, sir."

"Thoth? The god of wisdom, hmm? Let's see if you can live up to such a grand name, Transfer Trainee Thoth. Find me that unauthorized transfer in the next hour. I will send you the coordinates from where the subject was taken. You find me where she was sent. And do not utter a word of this to anyone, is that clear?"

"Yes, sir. Absolutely, sir." Thoth gulped.

"If your supervisors want to know what you are doing, tell them it is a training project under my orders. No one should bother you since the transfers are shut down. I will contact you again in one hour, and I expect you to have an answer for me."

Artemis shut the communication window before Thoth could say he needed more time than that. It was probably true, but Artemis didn't have more time to offer him. They needed answers, now.

As his last step before contacting Commander Griffin, Artemis made one more call.

"Yes?" the black-and-white cat grumbled, roused from sleep.

"Special Agent Buddy, your vast Earth experience is required for an urgent situation."

Buddy rolled over and stared into the monitor.

"What's happening, Artemis?" he asked, rubbing

the sleep from his eyes with the back of a paw. "Didn't they find the children?"

"Yes and no, so your help is needed. Prepare yourself and meet me in your brother's room as soon as you can. I'll explain it all then."

Buddy twitched his whiskers, but he nodded and switched off the monitor.

Not Earth again, he thought. *Fur balls.*

SNOWBALL SAW the orders come through. All transfers were shut down indefinitely. No one could come or go from Earth without special permission directly from the high commander. The note mentioned something about a system malfunction, but Snowball knew better. Nothing was wrong with the system. That was going to cause some slow down to his plan.

Snowball wished he had been at his transfer post instead of in his room. He could have delayed the shutdown. Now it was too late. From the small window on his computer where he was monitoring her, he saw Miss Fatty Cat's image.

"Snowball," she whispered, "I think they already

know what happened to Kimba. I heard Hiro warning whoever is watching her mirror. I didn't think she'd notice her sister missing until morning, but she did. Time is running out. You need to hurry and grab Hiro tonight while she sleeps. Hack into her mirror or something."

The fat cat looked around nervously and then jumped down from the sink with a loud thunk. She was right to be worried about being overheard, and Snowball hoped that no other agents were monitoring her mirror. Everyone had left their stations, so he guessed that he was the only one who heard her message.

He flexed his claws in frustration. They knew about Kimba. That was why the transfers had been shut down. The High Command was protecting Hiro. Thousands of agents were being delayed because of one stupid cat. It was a perfect example of everything that was wrong with the levels of cat importance on the ships. Everything came to a standstill because a high-level cat was in danger. Snowball doubted the reaction would be the same for a worker cat.

It was totally impossible to snatch Hiro now without revealing himself as a mole—a spy for the League For Cat Equality—hidden in the most trusted ranks of the high commander's staff. That part of the plan would have to be scratched.

His only hope now was if Kimba happened to have survived her visit to the tigers. If she were alive, they would still have a bargaining chip on their side. He would have to find a way to get himself back to headquarters so he could find out and try to move her to the hidden room Commander Horus had set up. How would he accomplish this without getting caught? He had no idea.

Chapter 12
ALONE

The sky was dark now except for the dim moonlight that fell ominously around the refuge. Kimba hadn't made contact with any people, but she had found an old cinder block next to a human building. It was hidden in some tall grass and was a perfect hiding spot. Wedging herself inside one of the holes, she hoped she could stay out of sight for the night.

She had seen a few more humans around the refuge after the animals were locked in their houses for the night. It seemed like a good idea to run to them for help, but they all had big, noisy, car-like machines. What if she got caught under a tire before they saw her? Others had huge water hoses and were cleaning out some of the areas near the largest building where the cats lived on concrete floors.

No thank you, she thought, watching the streams of pressurized water spray everywhere.

The cougars and lions and tigers in these cages near the human buildings were not locked up for the night, but they also didn't have the open, grassy areas to play in. They paced back and forth along the fencing or lounged on strange beds that looked like the top of the crisscross pies that Mama made for special occasions.

Mama, Kimba thought. *She probably hasn't even noticed that I'm missing yet.*

Her heart felt heavy at the memory of her safe home with the people who loved her. Right about now they would be curled up on the sofa watching TV together and chatting about the day. The scratchy cinder block was no substitute for her favorite dining room chair. How would she ever get back to them?

She watched and waited until dark. The humans had all left before she felt safe approaching them. Kimba wasn't really sure what the humans could do to help her get back home anyway. She didn't wear a collar with tags on it because she never went outside.

Once when The Big Black Beast ran off for a few

hours without his collar, Kimba had heard Mama talk about some kind of special computer chip that he had hidden in his fur. She promised the girls that it would help anyone who found him to know where he belonged. Kimba did not have one of those magical chips either.

From her hiding place in the cinder block, Kimba stared up at the dark night sky. Millions of stars twinkled down at her. Somewhere up in those stars her mother, the high commander, must be worried about her and trying to find her. Kimba knew that Artemis would never stop looking. But what if that wasn't enough?

Her stomach grumbled and made a sad wheezing noise. It had been a long time since breakfast, and transfers always left a cat feeling extra hungry. There was no one waiting on the other end of this transfer with a plate of fresh fish for her like there had been on the spaceship. She was lost and alone, and she would have to wait until morning to find some food. Now that it was dark, she hoped she didn't end up as someone else's dinner long before she found a meal for herself.

Kimba snuggled as far back into the cinder block as possible and tucked her head under her front leg.

The concrete of the block was rough and hard, and it smelled dank and dirty, but it could keep her safe through the night.

She thought of her nice warm home and hoped that Hiro was still there and safe with the family. She couldn't begin to imagine how terrified her timid sister would be if she were wandering around the refuge on her own. Or if she were someplace worse.

At least it isn't freezing or terribly hot or raining or something like that, she thought. *It could certainly be a lot worse.*

A high-pitched yipping echoed through the mountains around her. Without even knowing why, every hair on her body stood up as high as it could in the cramped space. Her ears and nose flushed pink, and all of her senses went on full alert. More yipping and two or three howls echoed from another direction. Whatever creature it was, instincts deep in her soul told Kimba that it was not good for a little white cat who was lost in the Ozark Mountains.

They won't come so near the human buildings, she convinced herself. She really hoped they wouldn't, but she tried to snuggle even deeper into her hiding place, just in case.

Chapter 13
TRAITOR IN OUR RANKS

As Buddy rounded the corner to his brother's quarters, he saw Special Agent Artemis waiting for him in the hallway outside the door. He greeted Artemis with a simple nod of the head.

"The high commander is still away at a meeting of the High Council," Artemis said. "As far as she knows, Kimba and Hiro have been found and are safe. I don't want to let her know what is really happening until we have additional information and a plan in place."

"So we were wrong? They have not been found?" Buddy asked.

Artemis surveyed the empty hallways with narrowed eyes and flattened ears.

"Let's talk inside. The commander will need an update as well."

Artemis scratched three times on the red doorway. He paused, then he scratched twice more. Commander Griffin opened the door, ears back. Noticing his brother, his posture relaxed.

"Hey, Bud," he said.

"Hey, Grif," Buddy responded, blinking slowly. "Good to see you again."

"Greetings, Special Agent Artemis," Griffin added with a quick nod. "Hurry, come in. She's not back yet, but we don't have much time. The old ones on the High Council must be getting tired."

The three cats settled in on the large pillows that covered the floor of Felicity and Griffin's sleeping chambers. Sensing that his presence was more official than theirs, Artemis stayed upright and at attention.

"Thank you for alerting me right away about the problem," Griffin started. "What do we know so far? Start at the beginning so Buddy is up to speed."

"The situation is not entirely clear at this moment," Artemis said. "What we know for sure is that Agent Ebony marked a mirror at the family's new home. Her fur registration was spotted by a clever agent. I was able to locate Hiro in another room of the house and saw her sleeping. The humans might have been home, so I waited to make contact. There was no reason to risk rushing the process."

Artemis hesitated and lowered his ears.

"Special Agent Artemis, none of us had any reason to suspect that the rebels had located the children and certainly had no suspicion that they would take any action against them. No one is blaming you for following normal protocol."

Buddy glanced back and forth between the two of them, wondering what the rebels had to do with anything concerning Kimba and Hiro. What rebel cats had taken action?

Artemis pursed his whiskers and nodded. He was not so sure that the high commander would be as forgiving as her mate, even if she never said it out loud. He had been given the honor of protecting her two youngest children, but now . . .

"Thank you, Commander," Artemis continued. "I appreciate your kind words. And you are correct. There was no reason to suspect there was any risk. We had only just found the sisters ourselves."

"So what happened?" Buddy asked. "Is Kimba not in the same place as Hiro? I can't imagine

Mama . . ." He brushed his nose with one quick swipe of his paw. "I mean, the human female would not have sent her away just because they moved. Is the family all together in the new house?"

"Yes, the family is all there," Artemis continued. "At least we think so. But this evening Hiro appeared at the mirror in a frantic state. She reported that Kimba was missing from the house. The one they call Slinky, Agent Ebony's sister, saw a flash of light and watched Kimba vanish. I was unable to ask for more information because the human male came in and carried Hiro away."

"Ticks and fleas," Buddy grumbled. "I'm assuming none of us transferred her to the ship."

"No. It was a completely unauthorized transfer. There is no record of her arriving on the ship, so I can only assume that the rebels have sent her somewhere on Earth."

Commander Griffin sat up tall on his pillow.

"What is being done to recover my daughter?" he said with trepidation.

"I have a transfer employee searching for traces of Kimba's activity," Artemis assured him. "He is certain that he can find where she was sent if he is given enough time. We can only hope it will not take too long."

"Maybe we should bring Hiro to the ship," Buddy suggested.

"I have frozen all transfers," Artemis said. "She is safe on Earth for now, but I can't keep activity at a standstill for long without agents becoming angry. We need as much calm as possible."

"The rebels don't have transfer technology now, do they?" Buddy asked.

"Certainly not. They don't have access to anywhere on the ship large enough to build their own facility," Griffin said.

"So do you realize what that means?" Buddy said. "Someone on the high commander's staff made the transfer. It was done on our equipment and by one of our trusted members."

The three cats pondered this reality, ears and tails twitching.

"We need to lock down this entire operation. Clear headquarters of everyone but the most vital and trusted special agents," Griffin ordered. "The rebel traitor could be anyone."

"I know just who to put in place," Artemis said. "And I think we can trust that Thoth fellow who is looking for Kimba's transfer. He appears terrified of his own shadow. I'll find a senior transfer technician and get our best special agents. Do you suppose Medusa would consider coming up to the ship for a day or two? The high commander trusts her more than she trusts any of us, I think."

Griffin pursed his whiskers, but he nodded.

"If Felicity asks, Medusa will come," Buddy said. "I will arrange for a replacement double to fool her human."

"Felicity will be grateful that you are on top of the rescue efforts, but all of this news will be best coming directly from me," Griffin said. "We have not heard anything from the rebels yet? No ransom demands?"

"No, Commander."

"That is odd," he said. "If they have Kimba secured, why are they waiting?"

No one had any answers.

"Send the coordinates for the family's new home to my computer," Buddy said. "I'll get some plans organized and see if Medusa has learned anything that can help. Let me know as soon as you discover where Kimba was sent."

Artemis nodded and trotted out the door, leaving the brothers alone.

"He's going to send you to Earth to find her, isn't he?" Griffin said.

"Yep, I'm pretty sure that's his plan."

"Sorry about that, Bud. Last time was supposed to be, well, the last. And you just got back a week ago."

"It's okay," Buddy said. "If your children need me, I will be there. Just like I was before."

Kidnapped royal children and rogue rebel cats. I'm getting way too old for this nonsense, he thought.

Chapter 14
THOTH'S BAD NEWS

Moments after Artemis left, the red light on Griffin's computer went off. Opening the channel, he saw a young, nervous-looking tortie cat. He couldn't be more than thirty years old.

"Greetings, Commander Griffin," he stammered. "Is Special Agent Artemis still with you?"

"No, he is in route back to his station."

"Oh ... well ..."

"What is it, young one?"

"I'm Transfer Trainee Thoth, sir. Special Agent Artemis asked me to find an unauthorized transfer that happened this evening."

Buddy and Griffin were suddenly paying very close attention.

"Did you find it?"

"Yes, sir, I did," he continued, his ears back and his tail thrashing in anger.

"Well?" Griffin urged him.

"Maybe I should wait and tell Special Agent Artemis myself," he said, whiskers twitching.

"Do you realize that I am the commander of this ship?"

"Yes, sir," he barely squeaked, eyes wide.

"And that this is my daughter you have information about?"

Thoth swallowed hard, terrified to continue.

"I understand all of that perfectly," he managed to say. "But Special Agent Artemis was very clear that I was not to speak to anyone else. I probably shouldn't even have said why I needed to talk to him."

Griffin and Buddy exchanged knowing looks. Buddy's ears flicked. Griffin's eyes narrowed, but he had to admire the young one's determination and obedience. Artemis must have already suspected there was someone on the inside who was not to be trusted. Felicity did well in selecting him to monitor their children.

"Wait just one moment," Griffin said. He tapped

a button beside his computer and opened up the inter-ship communication speaker. "Special Agent Artemis, please report to the nearest secure computer station. I repeat: Artemis, please report to the nearest secure station."

Thoth twitched nervously as he waited, but he held his ground. Griffin and Buddy pretended to be very involved with tending to loose toenails. After only a minute, Artemis appeared on the split screen next to Thoth.

"Sorry for the delay," Artemis said. "I wanted to make it all the way back to my room so I could be assured of the terminal security. Ah, Transfer Trainee Thoth, do you have answers for us?"

"Yes, sir. Do I have your permission to speak freely in front of everyone here?"

Artemis flicked his whiskers in amusement, but he was grateful for the loyalty.

"Yes, Thoth, you may speak freely."

"Okay, sir, this is what I have found. At 6:08 this evening Earth time, a transfer was made from the house in question to a location on Earth just a few miles away."

"What location?" Griffin demanded.

"The map shows it to be a place called Turpentine Creek Wildlife Refuge," Thoth said, a lump settling in his throat.

The agents looked to each other for answers, but none knew what to say. All they understood was that Kimba being at a wildlife refuge wasn't good. A bit braver now, and knowing he had the answers they needed, Thoth continued.

"I took a moment to research this refuge before I contacted you, in case that would give us some helpful information toward rescuing Kimba."

He hesitated. They were not going to like what came next.

"This refuge is for lions and tigers and cougars and other large and small animals that have been rescued from humans who would not or could not care for them properly. It appears to be a giant cat zoo."

"Are you telling me my daughter has been literally dropped into the middle of a zoo?" Griffin asked.

"Sort of."

"What do you mean 'sort of'?" Griffin growled.

Thoth lowered his ears, but he knew the truth had to be told.

"Based on the coordinates of the transfer and

what I can see on our map of the area . . . I mean, I am still in training, so I could be wrong . . ."

"Say it, Thoth," Griffin managed between clenched teeth.

"From what I can tell, Kimba was dropped directly into the middle of one of the enclosures. It looks . . . it looks like they put her in with a tiger."

The fur on Griffin's entire body rose and his eyes narrowed into tiny slits. Buddy hunkered down next to him, and Artemis lowered his ears as far as they could go.

"I will find her, Griffin," Buddy whispered.

"Find her, and then find whoever did this. He will be lucky if he lives long enough to regret it."

Rebel Commander Horus kicked the door shut behind her. They had been so close to achieving their goal, and now the whole operation was nothing short of a disaster. Headquarters had been cleared of all personnel. The transfer system was shut down, and no one seemed to have any idea what was really going on.

She slammed her paw down on the communication button and glared at the screen. Snowball's image appeared, his ears flat and his bright-green eyes wide.

"Yes, Commander Horus?"

"Do you have Kimba in hand yet?" she demanded.

"No, ma'am," Snowball admitted. "They noticed she was gone and shut down all of the transfer stations on the whole ship before I could move her to a more secure location."

Horus stiffened her whiskers and puffed her thrashing tail.

"Do you realize that you have ruined this whole plan with your hasty actions?"

Snowball lowered his eyes, hoping to avoid the reprimand he knew he deserved.

"Because you couldn't wait a couple of hours to talk with the League Commanders, our major bargaining tools are out of our reach. If they should recover Kimba, her security will be doubled, if not tripled. It's possible you could have been compromised with that unauthorized transfer. If you are caught, decades of planning and placement within the high commander's staff will be for nothing."

"I understand," Snowball said.

"I'm not sure you really do!" she growled. "Have you thought about what will happen if Kimba is *never* recovered? What if she has died on Earth with no way to reclaim her essential being?"

Snowball glanced back up at Horus in shock.

"The League will be guilty of murder," she continued. "The League for Cat Equality will be blamed for the death of the high commander's daughter in only the second year of her life. The High Command will have no problem rallying every cat on every ship to find each and every one of us and rout us out. We will be seen as nothing more than terrorists, instead of warriors for equality and justice."

"You know I didn't mean for this to happen," Snowball insisted. "I thought I was just taking advantage of a perfect opportunity."

"That may be true, but the League Council has already met to determine what must happen next."

"Whatever they ask of me, you know I will do it," Snowball said, shifting uneasily in his seat.

"That is good to hear. They have voted to disavow you."

"Disavow?" Snowball gasped, his whole body crumpling into a ball.

"That is correct," Horus said. "If you are caught,

when you are caught, the League will offer you no protection or support. We will deny having any part of your plan or actions. If it comes down to that, we will even turn you over to the High Council as a traitor. Whatever must be done to protect the values and integrity of the League is all that matters now. You and Agent Ebony and anyone who helped you are on your own and will have to suffer whatever punishments the high commander sees fit."

"I understand." Snowball sighed.

He had known Horus long before anyone attached the title of rebel commander to her name. Snowball knew there was no point in arguing.

"Find Kimba for them," Horus suggested, "and save your own pelt. That is your only option. And that is the end of this conversation."

The communication window abruptly shut, leaving Snowball to face his own fate. He didn't have a chance to tell her that Special Agent Artemis had already called for his assistance as a trusted transfer operations specialist. He was going to have to do whatever it took to find Kimba and make this whole mess go away. He only hoped that would be enough.

Chapter 15
TRUSTED ALLIES

When Buddy arrived at his work station at headquarters, the coordinates for the family house and the refuge were already waiting for him. Telling the high commander about Kimba's abduction had gone about as well as could be expected.

The High Council meeting ended immediately, and Felicity and Griffin were now with him at headquarters to clear out all non-essential cats and begin the rescue operation. Buddy just needed to get the trusted agents in place before he transferred down to Earth to search for his niece.

He tapped into the mirror and saw Hiro, safe and sleeping on her pillow again. He split the computer screen and tapped into Medusa's mirror as well. The room was dark, but his eyes rapidly adjusted. He spotted her outline as she sat in the window, gazing out at the front yard. No one else was in the room, so he took a chance.

"Greetings, Special Agent Medusa Gloriosa," he whispered without showing himself.

She turned to face him, slowly and dramatically.

"Greetings, Special Agent Buddy," she said. "It's all right. Mummy isn't home yet. She was dressed up beautifully when she left, so she must be on a date. We will see her car lights when she arrives."

Buddy opened up the full communication window. The lights from his side cast an eerie glow around the dark living room.

"Did you discover any news about the missing cats?" he asked.

"No," she said. "There are no new cats on my street. Everything is just the same as it was before. Except that it's summertime, so the motorcycles are rumbling around everywhere. They hurt my poor ears," she whined.

"Sorry about that," he said. "At least you have a cozy, safe house to live in."

Medusa shook her head and let her fur fall majestically.

"As if I would live anywhere else on this planet."

"Naturally," Buddy said. "Well, we have found the two cats who are missing, but one of them has been transferred out of the house to another location in town. We fear that the rebels are behind this transfer, but we have not heard from them yet. Their plan may be to simply abandon her there."

He pulled up the maps of the area on the mirror below him showing her location, the family house, and where Kimba had been dropped.

"You are this X, Medusa. The new home for our missing family is this X. And the spot where the high commander's daughter was dropped is this X."

She squinched her nose and flexed her whiskers.

"Very nice," she mumbled, wondering what any of this had to do with her.

"We are certain there is a spy deep in the high commander's staff. It is difficult to know whom to trust."

"Well, I would certainly never get involved with those nasty rebels. Freedom and equality for all cats? Humph."

The system on the ships had worked smoothly

for millions of years, and Medusa could see no reason to change it.

"The high commander knows you would not waste your time with the rebels, and she trusts you completely. She is asking for your help in finding her daughter."

Medusa puffed up at such direct praise from the high commander herself. Buddy believed he had her attention now, so he continued.

"This place Kimba has been sent, this Turpentine Creek Wildlife Refuge, have you ever heard of it?"

"Of course. Everyone in town has. Mummy goes to events there sometimes, and she enjoys looking at their Facebook photos on her computer. She says I am more beautiful than any of those tigers."

Buddy's eyes narrowed, but didn't react further.

"Do you suppose there are any mirrors that Kimba could find?" he asked. "If I go in after her, I'm not sure how to get us back home again. It seems to be awfully far away from the city, at least for two cats trying to walk. Kimba has not done any combat training here on the ship, so she is not prepared to handle coyotes or bobcats or other animals that may live along the way."

"Goodness, is she there in the dark all alone?"

Medusa shivered at the thought of it.

"Unfortunately, yes."

He didn't mention that Kimba had been transferred right into a tiger enclosure. His niece was a crafty girl. Buddy was certain she had gotten out. At least he hoped so.

"In our training," Medusa said, "we were always told to look for a human bathroom. Those areas almost always have mirrors. There were code names like Operation Broad Daylight or Emergency Recovery Protocol. If those in charge at headquarters knew the general location of an agent, they would monitor the bathroom mirrors in the area. It's all basic agent training."

"Kimba has not been through any agent training," he admitted. "She is a brand-new cat, born on Earth to the high commander."

Medusa squinched her nose again. She did not approve of sloppy things like having babies at the wrong time and place. An important cat shouldn't be allowed to stay on Earth without some training. It all seemed very obvious to her. Unsure of Buddy's connections to the royal family, Medusa was careful with her response. No intelligent agent cat wanted to upset the high commander.

"I see," she said. "So, if I understand this all correctly, the youngest child of the high commander, who has no training whatsoever, has been allowed to remain on Earth and has now been transferred into a highly dangerous situation by a spy for the League For Cat Equality who works directly for the high commander."

Buddy nodded with regret. Medusa's ears twitched.

Very sloppy, she thought, *but even the smartest of us do silly things when our children are involved.*

"That is quite a messy problem," she said.

"I agree, but our only concern at this moment is to rescue Kimba and ensure that Hiro remains safe. Like I said, we have not had any demands from the League For Cat Equality, and we fear that they are not in control of the situation either. Kimba is simply out there on her own."

"And even if she finds a mirror and tries to communicate . . . well, she could end up talking with that spy and not even know it."

"This is true," he admitted. "That is why we are contacting you."

He waited for her reaction. Medusa didn't flinch. She knew she had the advantage in this situation and was not going to agree to anything too soon.

"The high commander has requested that you return to the ship," he continued, "just for a brief time, to help monitor all of the mirrors that Kimba might contact."

"Is there no one on the ship who you can trust as much as me?" she said coyly.

"Not many." Buddy sighed. "And they are already involved in taking shifts and monitoring Hiro to ensure her continued safety. You would be working directly with Special Agent Artemis and the high commander herself."

That was all very impressive to the fancy cat. She blinked her eyes slowly with pride and dignity.

"A reasonable double will be placed in your home so your human doesn't worry," he continued. "She couldn't begin to take your place for long, but during the night your human should not become suspicious."

"Take my place, indeed," Medusa said. "Mummy would know immediately. Who could replace ME?"

"As I said, it is only temporary. But we do need to move fast."

"Fine," she agreed. "But only for the high

commander and out of respect for our two hundred years of friendship. I will help her find her daughter."

"Excellent," Buddy said, thoroughly relieved. "Prepare yourself for transfer to the ship."

Medusa shook herself all over, used the back of her paw to wipe her face clean, stood up tall, and sighed dramatically.

"Okay, I am ready."

Buddy nodded to Artemis, standing across the room at the platform with Senior Transfer Operations Specialist Snowball. The system was unlocked to allow for the transfer, and Medusa was with them in the room a moment later. When she arrived, she found herself facing another Himalayan cat, not nearly as beautiful as she was, but acceptable.

"That should fool Mummy for a short while," she admitted.

The two cats traded places, and the double nodded that she was ready. There was a bright flash of light, and then she was gone.

"Well then," Medusa said, "let's get started."

Chapter 16
DISTURBED SLEEP

Miss Fatty Cat had a fitful sleep. It was impossible to get comfortable. She rolled from her back to her side and over again without finding peace. All her tossing and turning made Leia stir.

"Come here, baby." The girl sighed, dragging the fat cat across the bed and tucking her up under her arm. "Cuddle with me, and go to sleep."

Cuddling was not what Miss Fatty Cat had in mind, but the girl held on tight. Giving up, the cat stared at the shadows on the wall. Her hopes to get rid of the sisters were not going as planned. She wasn't sure what Snowball and the League were up to, but Hiro was still home at bedtime. Something must have gone wrong.

Had they been caught? Was the high commander refusing to negotiate? Could any of this be traced back to her? She wished she hadn't talked through the mirror without knowing who might be on the other end. What if a loyal agent had been listening?

She was locked in the bedroom until morning, so her answers would just have to wait. She closed her eyes and tried to sleep, but visions of being called before the High Council as a traitor plagued her thoughts.

"I'm not part of the rebel group," she imagined pleading. "I just wanted the sisters out of the house so I could be the favorite."

Her tail puffed and her claws flexed at the thought of trying to explain that to the high commander.

Hiro couldn't sleep either. She hopped down from her special bed and joined Daddy on the big bed. Hiro buried her face deep into the blankets.

Mama and Daddy still had not noticed that

Kimba was missing. With empty boxes everywhere and so much to do, even Mama had not looked for her.

They don't understand, she thought. *They don't realize that she can be grabbed right from under their noses. They just think she's sleeping somewhere.*

Hiro tried to rest as her tail thrashed and her back twitched with worry. Kimba was brave and strong, but she was still only two years old. Why couldn't the rebels just pick on someone else?

What have they done with Kimba? she fretted. *What if she never comes back?*

That thought was more than the little tuxedo cat could bear. She wrapped her legs around Daddy's arm and tried not to think of anything else.

Kimba woke to a bone-chilling sound. It took her a moment to remember where she was, but then the terrifying noise vibrated through the cinder block and up into her body once again.

Blinking against the darkness, Kimba sniffed the air. The strong odors of humans and big cats and grizzly bear still surrounded her. Nothing had changed since she fell asleep. The sound came again, this time from her other side. It was low and deep and made her spine tingle.

Peeking out from her hiding place, Kimba could barely make out the small caged areas across the walkway from her. Standing in the middle of one was an enormous male lion with a mane so thick Kimba wasn't sure how he was able to hold his head up at all.

He opened his mouth, baring razor-sharp fangs, and the noise poured out of him. His whole body lurched with the effort, but his mouth looked like he was ready to whistle.

"Hooorrrr, hooorrrr, hooorrrr," echoed away into the night.

"Hooorrrr, hooorrrr, hooorrrr," came the low, rumbling roar, caroling in return from another part of the refuge.

"Hah-rooo," a dog-like howl echoed back from another corner. "Yip, yip, yip, hah-rooo."

The lion whoofed loudly, content that all was well across his domain, and then plopped back down on his big crisscross bed.

A white tiger in a nearby cage paced back and forth in the dark. An agitated rhythm to his steps, he huffed as he reached each corner and was forced to change directions.

Thump, thump, thump, thump, huff. Thump, thump, thump, thump, huff. On and on. Over and over.

The gentle summer winds blew, and the fencing creaked and groaned as it shifted in the breeze. Kimba thought she even heard something that sounded like a monkey farther in the distance.

"Ooohoo, oohoo, oohoo." Soft grunts sounded in the darkness.

Kimba's empty tummy grumbled and moaned in response.

It's going to be a long night. She sighed. *Once the humans come back in the morning, I'm going to have to turn myself over to them. This is no place for a tiny house cat.*

Willy the lion, in his early days at Turpentine Creek. Later he had a large grassy enclosure to play with his boomer ball and carolled across the refuge to let everyone know he was there. It was a most impressive sound.

Chapter 17
WHERE'S KIMBA?

The beeping of Leia's alarm clock startled Miss Fatty Cat out of her dreams. She sighed and rolled over, pushing her paws against Leia's unmoving body.

"Okay, okay," the girl mumbled and hit the snooze button. "A few more minutes."

Knowing that this was likely to happen several more times before her owner actually got up and let her out of the bedroom, the fat cat tried to return to the happy place she had found in her sleep.

She had been dreaming about being the only cat in the whole house. Well, her sister Slinky was there, but she didn't really count. Kimba and Hiro were gone, and everyone in the house doted on Miss Fatty Cat instead.

Mama would bring her bowls of specially prepared meals that she would not have to share with anyone. Daddy would tell her that she was beautiful and ask her to sit next to him on the sofa. Leia wouldn't be allowed to lock her in the bedroom or make her play dress-up, and she could go anywhere and do anything she pleased.

The beeping of the alarm started again, reminding her that Kimba and Hiro were the darlings of the house, not her. She grumbled and tucked her head under her leg. When she was awake, Miss Fatty Cat was going to have to deal with what had happened to Kimba, whether Hiro was still in the house or not, and even if Snowball had been caught. Dreams were better.

Hiro heard Daddy's alarm clock, and she cracked one eye open. The sun was up, but just barely. She waited patiently, pretending to still be asleep, until Daddy got up and opened the bedroom door. Kimba was always nearby in the morning, hoping for some fresh water from the sink. This morning there were only noises from Leia's room as she got ready for the day.

Hiro stared at the bathroom mirror, but there was no way to get answers from the Cats in the Mirror right now. She wandered across the big bed to the far side at the bottom. From there, she could see out of the bedroom door.

"Hiro, not yet," Mama mumbled as she shifted her feet out from under the cat's body.

Hiro hunkered down and watched out the door for any sign of Kimba. Maybe she had come back during the night and was still asleep somewhere in the house.

As Hiro considered heading out in search of her sister, The Big Black Beast burst full speed through the bedroom door. His ears flopped, and his tail lashed around as if it were trying to launch him into space. Sliding to a stop just inches from Hiro, he flashed her a doggie smile. A bit of drool escaped from one side of his flapping jowls.

"Good Morning, Kitty Cat!" he said in a cheery voice.

Hiro was in no mood for him today.

"Get Out! Get Out! Get Out!" she hissed at him, smacking at his nose with her claws extended.

The Beast yelped and ran from the room, searching for comfort from Daddy. Mama moaned again and rolled over, knocking Hiro off the bed with her feet.

"It's too early," she grumbled. "Go-lie-down-Max."

Hiro pouted on the floor next to the bed for a minute, then she spotted Miss Fatty Cat walking out of Leia's room.

"Hey," she whispered. "Have you seen Kimba?"

Miss Fatty Cat froze and stared at Hiro with wide eyes, ears laid back. Her whiskers twitched nervously, and her tail puffed and thrashed from side to side.

"Why would I know where your sister is?" she spat out. "It's not my job to watch her."

"Sheesh, fine," Hiro said. "I just thought you might have seen her this morning."

"No," the fat cat said. "Leave me alone. I didn't talk to any old Cats in the Mirror. You're crazy." She hissed and slunk back into Leia's room and under the bed.

That was weird, Hiro thought. Miss Fatty Cat was rarely pleasant, but Hiro had never seen her that upset. *And what was that about Cats in the Mirror?*

Daddy came back in the room and distracted her thoughts.

"Did Kimba come in here?" he asked Mama.

She just grumbled and pulled the covers up over her head. Daddy chuckled and looked down at Hiro.

"Guess she wouldn't know," he said. "Leia, have you seen Kimba this morning?"

"Nope," she called back. "She usually hangs out in the bathroom with me, but I haven't seen her at all this morning. She wasn't around last night either."

That got Daddy thinking, and Mama pulled the covers off her head.

"What did she say about Kimba?" she asked.

"It just seems like a long time since anyone has seen her. Did you hear her singing last night? There aren't any toys on the floor out here either."

"Not that I remember," Mama said, rubbing sleep from her eyes. "But she's got to be around here somewhere."

"Yeah," Daddy said, but he didn't seem sure.

"She's probably just hiding. I'll look for her in a little while," Mama mumbled, flopping the covers back over her head.

Hiro followed Daddy into the bathroom and jumped up on the counter. It was pretty clear now that Kimba had not come back during the night. She was still lost.

"They are starting to worry about her," she said to the mirror and to whatever cat might be listening.

"Good morning to you too." Daddy laughed, not understanding her true words.

As soon as Leia was done in the bathroom, Miss Fatty Cat headed for the mirror to see where things stood. Just to be safe, she pushed the bathroom door almost closed behind her. Then she jumped up on the sink and hoped for a miracle.

"Greetings, Snowball," she whispered to the mirror that shone back her own reflection. She wasn't just going to report randomly this time. If he wasn't there, she would keep quiet.

The mirror lit up with the image of her rebel contact, his green eyes wide.

"Greetings, Agent Ebony," he whispered. "Is the house empty already?"

"Mama is still in bed," she assured him, "and Daddy and Leia are playing outside with The Beast. Mindy won't be up for hours, so we have a few minutes to talk. How long until you transfer Hiro out? Is the High Council listening to your demands?"

Snowball twitched his nose, and his tail swept across the back of his seat. He was all alone in his quarters for a short nap break before the operation began, but he imagined the walls might have ears. He leaned in close and spoke in a low voice.

"Operation Persuasion has not come together as we had expected," he admitted.

"What's the problem?" she asked. "You have Kimba."

"Well, not exactly," Snowball said.

"Then what exactly is the situation?" she demanded.

"Kimba was transferred out of the house, but I lost track of her once I put her down in the tiger cage."

Miss Fatty Cat stared at the mirror in silence for what seemed like an eternity to Snowball.

"Are you telling me you *lost her*?" she finally asked. "You lost the high commander's daughter?"

"That is correct."

"How could you just lose her like that? The high commander is going to freak out. You know that, don't you? When she finds out—"

"They already know most of it," he interrupted. "They just don't know who did it."

Miss Fatty Cat glanced at the door warily. This was not at all what she thought she was getting into. All Snowball was supposed to do was get the sisters out of her house. He was going to snatch Kimba and Hiro and hold them hostage for a while. The High Council would meet some of the League's demands, and the royal sisters would be returned to the ship. They would never be allowed back to Earth again. It seemed all very simple. Then she started to think through exactly what Snowball had told her.

"Wait, what did you say about a tiger cage?"

"I transferred Kimba into a tiger cage at a wildlife rescue park near your house. I just meant to dump her nearby somewhere and recover her later when I could think of a better place."

"Are you saying Kimba could be *dead*?"

Snowball gulped and nodded slowly. Miss Fatty Cat laid back her ears and her eyes narrowed.

"What pile of fleas have you gotten me mixed up in?" she hissed. "The high commander will never let this rest. She will comb through every record and every transfer until she finds out exactly what happened."

He nodded again.

"You need to find that stupid little cat and find her NOW! If she is dead . . ."

She didn't need to say the words out loud. They both knew what the consequences would be. Kidnapping and her safe return were one thing. Murder was quite another.

"I'll keep you updated on activities from here, Agent Ebony," Snowball assured her. "It's tricky right now, but I'll do my best."

"No," she said, "do not contact me again. This was a mistake. A horrible mistake. I'm not going to lose my honor, my rank, and frankly at this point I need to worry about all nine of my lives over this stupid operation. Keep me out of it. If you are caught, I will deny everything."

With that, Miss Fatty Cat thumped down from the sink, pushed the door open with her nose, and waddled to hide under Leia's bed.

Snowball considered calling her back, but he understood her fears. Besides, he didn't really need her from that point on. There was no way the League was going to try to kidnap Hiro now.

Snowball turned off his computer, being sure to delete any evidence of his contact with Agent Ebony in her Earth home. Fortunately, he was the most senior and trusted transfer specialist on the ship. Commander Griffin was allowing him to help with the rescue operation. He was the last person the High Command would ever suspect.

Chapter 18
OPERATION REFUGE RESCUE

When Snowball returned to the control room at headquarters, the high commander was still there with her most trusted allies: Griffin, Buddy, Regalus, Medusa, and Artemis. The rest of the room was vacant and silent. All other computers were shut down. It was so empty that the padded footsteps of the fluffy white cat echoed off the black tile floors and around the vast room.

Special Agent Medusa was manning one computer terminal, watching the mirror in an employee break room at Turpentine Creek Wildlife Refuge. Special Agent Artemis was observing the bathroom mirrors there. Special Agent Regalus was monitoring another mirror, watching Hiro rest uneasily on her pillow in the humans' bedroom. Buddy, Griffin, and Felicity were busy discussing the rescue plan.

"Commander?" Regalus called out, noticing the presence of the transfer technician.

"He's okay," Commander Griffin signaled back. Felicity shot him a questioning look. "Well, we need someone to run the transfer. Snowball has been on your staff far longer than anyone else, and his records are totally clean. No connection to the rebels has ever been suspected. Thoth doesn't have the training to do the process all by himself, and he's still busy trying to discover who actually made that unauthorized transfer."

Felicity pursed her whiskers, but she knew her mate was right. She glanced over at the nervous transfer trainee, working at his station. The sooner he found the answer to who the traitor was, the better.

"If only the scans would pick up Kimba's fur registry." Felicity sighed. "Maybe she is just hiding, and we can't see her. Or maybe she is inside of a building."

Griffin could think of a few other, nastier reasons why the scans didn't find any evidence of Kimba, but he kept those thoughts to himself. Buddy would find her, one way or another.

Snowball manned his position at the transfer controls. Thoth didn't appear to be any closer to finding the source of the unauthorized transfer, and Snowball was grateful he had coded and hidden it well. The young one shouldn't be able to crack it.

He watched as Griffin and Buddy discussed the maps of the refuge and what paths Buddy should follow when he arrived. Snowball strained and twisted his ears to hear their plans. Even his strong cat hearing could not catch everything.

"Start out here," Commander Griffin said, tapping his claw on a location outside the enclosure where Kimba had been dropped. "Look around carefully, and be sure to check for any . . ." He whispered so the high commander couldn't hear him. "Check for any remains."

Buddy nodded his understanding, with a tentative glance at Kimba's mother. She was distracted at the moment by observing Thoth, and Buddy was grateful.

"I may be able to get information from whatever creature is living in that cage as well," Buddy said. "Then I'll follow this human path up to the main buildings. I can make contact with Artemis through the bathroom mirror at that point to see if you have any updates. Then I can begin to explore the more wooded areas around the refuge if necessary."

"High Commander," Regalus called, "Hiro is coming into the bathroom. I have not seen a human for quite a while, so the house may be empty. Her audio channel is already open."

Felicity and Griffin rushed over to join him, and they watched through the mirror as Hiro jumped up onto the counter and looked directly at them.

"Greetings," Hiro said, tapping the mirror with one paw. "Is anyone there? Have you found Kimba yet?"

Regalus opened up the audio on their side as well.

"Is it safe to communicate?" he asked. "Are the humans gone?"

"They are all outside working in the front yard before it gets too hot. Daddy is riding the big tractor around. We have to be careful, but it is safe for now. Have you found her?"

Regalus opened the full communication window, and Hiro was greeted by the familiar face of her first Cat in the Mirror contact, along with both of her parents. She lowered her ears, and her tail thrashed violently. Seeing all three of them was not a good sign, and her memories of Special Agent Regalus made her hackles rise.

"Greetings, Hiro," Regalus said. "It has been a long time."

"Greetings, Regalus," she said hesitantly. "Are you helping to find my sister?"

"My main task is to monitor you during this time of crisis and to be sure you stay informed and safe."

"Okay," she said, unsure if that was comforting or not.

"Hiro," High Commander Felicity said, "we know where Kimba was transferred to. At this time, we are not exactly sure where she is. Your uncle is going to come back down to Earth to search for her and bring her home."

"My uncle?" Hiro said.

"Yes, we have mentioned him several times before," Commander Griffin said. "My brother, Special Agent Buddy."

Hiro's eyes widened. *Buddy?* Her back began to twitch, and her tail began to act up so much she wasn't sure how long she could stand it.

"Buddy is my uncle?" she asked. "Is Buddy there on the ship?"

"Yes, he is here with us and has been for several days. You were safe in your home there on Earth, and we felt confident in allowing him to end his mission and return home to the ship."

It was nice to have some answers about where Buddy had ended up. He was kind of a grumpy old cat, but she was glad he was all right.

"Do Mama and Daddy know where Buddy is? Not on the ship, of course. I mean, do they think Buddy ran off again or that he died?"

"A few days before the move, the adult humans noticed that he was not doing well, and they took him to the vet," her mother said. "It was all very calm and peaceful, though the human female cried quite a lot. I was surprised how attached she was to him. We recovered his essence easily, and that was supposed to be the end of his trips to Earth."

"But he will come back to find Kimba?"

"Yes, Hiro. He will come back to find Kimba."

Hiro tried to relax. She trusted that the wild-looking outdoor cat knew his way around, but it was awful to think that Kimba was lost somewhere in the big wide world.

"Am I safe here?" she finally asked. "Do I have to come up to the ship again? I really don't want to leave Daddy, but I even more don't want to get kidnapped by the rebels. I will do whatever you tell me to."

"That is very brave of you, My Daughter," her mother said with a sense of pride, "but we are not allowing any transfers. You are safe where you are. Regalus will continue to supervise your situation. Stay in view of the mirror as much as you can today. Then we will be assured that you are safe."

"It's time to start the recovery operation," Griffin said in a low voice.

Hiro nodded and blinked slowly at her parents.

"I will go back to my bed and stay where you can see me," she said. "Please bring my sister home to me."

Her mother nodded in return and closed the communication window.

"Keep watch," she told Regalus, "and leave the audio open on her side in case the humans say something important. They are already beginning to wonder where Kimba is."

"True," he admitted, "and it can't be too long before the female goes looking for her in earnest."

"Then let's get this started," she said, nodding across the room at Buddy.

Buddy climbed up onto the transfer platform and sat straight and tall. He had lost count of how many times he had completed this process over his many Earth-lives, but every time it was a bit of a risk. He never got lazy or inattentive. Transfers were serious business, and he was prepared.

"Do you have the coordinates, Snowball?" Griffin asked.

"Yes, sir," Snowball responded, not adding that he had known them longer than anyone else in the room.

"Buddy, this should put you down right in front of the enclosure where Kimba was dropped. The sun is up, but it is early yet so there shouldn't be many humans around. Be safe, Brother."

Buddy nodded and closed his eyes, relaxing his entire body. Snowball engaged the system, making necessary adjustments for Buddy's size and age and the distance of the transfer. Successful transfers were an art as well as a science.

Trainee Thoth craned his neck and carefully watched Snowball's every move. Was he suspicious or just trying to learn? Snowball made sure everything was perfect, and then he engaged the transfer. There was a bright light, and Buddy disappeared.

The high commander sighed. It would take time for Buddy to find answers, but she had one more card to play before she gave up hope. Sitting down at the nearest computer station, Felicity clicked and tapped for several minutes before she found the exact link she needed. An old familiar face appeared on her screen.

"Greetings, Horus," she said between clenched teeth.

"Greetings, Felicity," Horus returned with even less enthusiasm.

The fur along the high commander's spine and tail bristled at the rebel's blatant refusal to use her official title, but history had taught her to expect nothing more.

"I'm sure you know why I'm calling," she said.

"No, I haven't got the faintest idea why you would want to communicate with me," Horus snarled back. "Until you and the High Council are willing to hear even the smallest of my new ideas, I have nothing to say to you."

"This goes beyond revolutionary and political agendas." She tried not to hiss, but the impulse was building in her throat. "This is about the kidnapping and attempted murder of my youngest daughter."

Horus's eyes narrowed, and her ears laid back flat. She was not going to step into that dirty litter.

"I have no idea what you are talking about," Horus said.

"Really?" Felicity spat. "The League For Cat Equality is not going to claim this major victory over oppression? You're going to let someone else take the credit for this crafty move?"

Horus knew what her old rival was up to, but she had no intention of chasing that mouse.

"I have nothing to do with whatever is going on in your family, and the League would never stoop so low as to commit murder. Our cause can stand on its own four paws. Justice will prevail without any cheap tricks or kidnapping, much less murder. How would killing your daughter help further our goals?"

The high commander knew that the explanation made perfect sense, but there was no other group to blame.

"We will find out who did this, Horus," she stressed. "We have already traced the transfer, and in the end, we will be able to determine who was involved."

"That is of no concern to me," she said. "I hope you locate the traitor and find your daughter. It's all a sad and messy business."

Felicity's ears twisted and turned, trying to find hidden meaning in the rebel's words.

"If that is all, I have much to attend to," Horus said, twitching her whiskers in annoyance.

Felicity nodded and closed the communication window without so much as a goodbye.

Big hairy fur balls, she thought.

Across the room, Snowball was thinking exactly the same thing.

When she ended her conversation with the Cats in the Mirror, Hiro headed straight for Leia's room. She knew she was supposed to stay in sight, but some of the things the fat cat had said earlier were still tickling around in Hiro's head. She probably should have told her parents about the fat cat's strange behavior, but she wanted to see what she could find out first.

Miss Fatty Cat was still hiding under the bed. Hiro hunkered down and glared at her.

"What do you know?" she demanded.

"Go away, baby kitty," Miss Fatty Cat growled. "I don't know anything."

"You're lying. I can tell. You're lying now just like when you said you didn't know about the Cats in the Mirror."

Miss Fatty Cat looked away from Hiro and past her toward the doorway. She could try to make a run for it and bowl Hiro over, but she sensed that the tuxedo cat was not going to give up that easily.

"Where's Kimba?" Hiro said. "You are acting too weird. I know you must be in on this. You've always hated us. What did you do?"

Miss Fatty Cat was nervous, and drool was pooling in her mouth. She smacked it down loudly. Hiro squinched her nose, but she did not move.

"Are you part of the rebel group?" Hiro continued. "Did you help them hurt Kimba?"

"I don't care anything about those upstart rebels and their silly demands," Miss Fatty Cat snarled, laying her ears back. "I am an agent!"

An agent? Miss Fatty Cat was an agent like Artemis and all of those cats she had grown to trust? It had to be true, or the cat wouldn't even know what an agent was. The high commander must know that

Miss Fatty Cat was an agent. Why hadn't she told them?

Glaring back at the fat cat under the bed, Hiro tried to set those worries aside for now. This agent knew more than she was admitting.

Miss Fatty Cat's tail thrashed. So did Hiro's, and her back began to twitch and jerk and demand attention. *Chase me*, her tail seemed to whisper. The fat cat waited for Hiro to be distracted enough that she could make a break for it. Hiro refused to play.

"Do you know where my sister is?" she asked again, tail puffed and swishing and ears flat.

"No. I have no idea where she is. Check Mama's office. And anyway, what do I care what happens to some spoiled, snotty, privileged little cat like Kimba? She doesn't even belong in this house. Neither of you do." She narrowed her eyes and kept her ears back in warning.

Fatty Cat wasn't lying. Well, not exactly. She really didn't know what Snowball had done with Kimba, but she was positive the white cat wasn't in Mama's office.

"If I ever find out that you helped hurt Kimba, you're going to be one sorry cat," Hiro growled.

"You can just run and tell Daddy," the fat cat

teased. "Poor baby kitties need the humans to fight their battles for them. You get to be the favorite of the house, and I am forced to wear doll clothes."

"What are you talking about?" Hiro said. "You have Leia, and she babies you just as much as Daddy babies me."

That idea surprised Miss Fatty Cat. She had seen Leia's behavior as annoying, but was the girl simply trying to spoil her?

"From where I sit," Hiro said, "you're a pampered little pet as much as any of the rest of us. Leia thinks you are the queen of the universe!"

"Hiro," Daddy called. "What's going on?"

He came around the corner and spotted the standoff.

"Well, that's not usually how these fights go." He smiled. "You tell her, Hiro. Better watch out, Miss Fatty Cat. She's getting big enough to take you on."

He scooped up Hiro, and she spat angry words over his shoulder.

"I can take you now!"

"Better watch out for your next thawunking!" Fatty Cat growled back from under the bed.

Left alone, Miss Fatty Cat awkwardly swallowed another mouthful of angry drool and crawled out from under the bed. Heaving herself onto it, she tried to calm down.

This was more drama than she had counted on. Snowball promised to remove Kimba and Hiro quickly with no proof she had helped. Now it was just a big mess.

But then she started to consider what Hiro had said. *Am I just as spoiled as they are?*

Hiro was definitely the most spoiled cat in the house, but the other three were not far behind. She really did have her own giant pillow to sleep on, but she also liked this comfy chair.

Chapter 19
BUDDY TO THE RESCUE

Karma was startled from her morning daydreams by a bright flash of light next to her yard. She raised her head out of the grass to see if it was Kimba again or maybe the sister she had mentioned. Instead, she noticed a longhaired black-and-white cat.

He was much larger than Kimba, but still tiny compared to a liger. This cat was outside the fences, so Karma pulled herself to her feet and sauntered over to greet him. Buddy raised his eyes to meet hers without flinching.

Definitely not Kimba's sister, Karma realized. That cat did not look one bit scared.

"Greetings, Madam Lioness . . . um, er, Tigress," Buddy said, examining the cat's strange markings.

"My name is Karma," she told him. "And I am a liger. More formally called a ligress, I suppose."

Buddy blinked a few times as he thought back through his years of education and training.

"Yes, I have heard of a liger before, but I've never seen one face-to-face. It is an honor to meet you, Karma. I am Special Agent Buddy. I apologize for interrupting you, but I am looking for a small white cat, rather like myself. She would have arrived here yesterday around dinnertime. Did you happen to see her?"

He hoped that was all that Karma had done.

"Why, yes, I did see her. She appeared in my yard, right in front of my face, like you just did."

"I am so sorry for that intrusion," Buddy said. "She didn't mean to bother you."

"Oh, she was no bother. It was nice to have a little something interesting happen. It would have been better to visit longer, but my brother might not have cared for having her here. I sent her up the hill to where the humans stay."

Buddy's whole body relaxed with relief. Kimba

had made it past this huge cat unharmed. Of course, that was many hours ago.

"Could you please point me in that direction as well?" he asked Karma.

"Just follow the road up that way," she motioned with her enormous velveted paw. "It is still pretty early, but some of the humans have already arrived to let us into our yards and serve breakfast."

"Thank you so much," Buddy said and bowed his head. "I'm so grateful for your kind assistance."

He started to walk up the hill, but he paused when Karma called after him.

"Wait a minute, please. Can you tell me where you two came from? Will there be more of you? This is really no place for tiny cats like you and Kimba."

"I couldn't agree with you more, Karma the ligress," he said. "This is not where we belong."

He debated how to make a quick explanation. It was a complicated story that involved how her ancestors got to Earth as well. There wasn't time to tell Karma everything she wanted to know.

"The simple answer is that I have spent many, many years on Earth, but my home is on a large spaceship up in the sky. As high as the stars."

Karma gazed up at the blue sky above her and

then back down at Buddy. She tipped her head and narrowed her eyes.

"I know it doesn't make sense to you." He sighed. "But I must get Kimba back to that ship as soon as possible. I don't have time to explain. But in gratitude for your help and for sparing Kimba's life, once my mission is done, I will see to it that someone returns to you and answers all of your questions. There are many things about your heritage that you don't understand."

Karma flexed her thick whiskers and blinked slowly at the small cat.

"I will watch for the flash of light," she said.

Buddy nodded his head again and ran up the hill full speed, calling for Kimba and listening for any response. He had been through every combat and wildlife training available to an agent and had faced some of those creatures in real life on Earth. Morning was not a very dangerous time to be out and about, and there was no time for hiding in the grass. Lions and tigers along his path raised their heads and turned to stare.

"Kimba?" he called. "Kimba, are you here?"

Racing past several more large enclosures, Buddy headed up the steep hill that ran beside the grizzly bear's home. He squeezed under the same fence Kimba had and trotted past the enclosure. Bam Bam was foraging around his territory for fruits and nuts that the keepers had hidden. He snuffled around his yard and did not even notice the black-and-white cat.

Buddy slowed his pace and lowered his voice as he approached the human buildings. He didn't have time to play any human "here, kitty kitty" games. The people were only of use if they could bring him to Kimba or get her to a mirror.

"Kimba?" he whispered as he searched the area for a good hiding place.

But there was no answer.

Kimba gazed out the large window in the ship's main hallway as stars twinkled in the distance. Cats of all shapes and sizes strode past her, avoiding eye contact and being sure to look very busy.

"High Commander Kimba?" the Siamese cat approached her and bowed his head.

"Yes, Special Agent Artemis, what do you need?"

she said, annoyed that he had disturbed her thoughts.

"High Commander Kimba, the High Command needs your opinion on a matter of grave importance to the safety of cats everywhere in the universe," he said. "The High Council cannot proceed without your input."

Kimba straightened up tall and nodded. She took one last glance out the window, back at the stars and the tiny blue dot of Earth in the distance. Life had been easier during her days on the planet as a pampered house cat, but now she had big, important, universe-saving decisions to make.

She turned to follow Artemis toward the High Council chamber, but a voice called her from the other direction.

"Kimba?"

It was a voice she recognized, but she was still a bit annoyed that he didn't address her correctly and use her official title.

That's High Commander Kimba to you, she thought.

"Kimba?" the familiar voice called again.

Blinking her eyes against the bright sunlight, Kimba roused from her dream. There was no ship.

She was certainly not high commander. The strange whoofing and snuffling of big cats all around her brought her back to her senses, and she heard the faint gravelly voice call again from somewhere in the tall grass.

"Kimba? Are you here?"

"Yes," she called back. "Over here by the building."

She poked her head out of the cinder block and saw an enormous black-and-white cat bounding toward her.

"Father?" she said.

The cat landed directly in front of her and hunkered down, his breathing heavy.

"No, Kimba. It's me. Buddy."

"How in the world did you get here?" she asked.

"We traced the rebel's transfer here. Your parents sent me to find you before someone else does."

"They know where I am?" she said, relieved.

"Yes, but we were not sure if you were still alive after being dropped into the liger cage and spending the night on your own with no training."

Kimba swallowed hard. Not still being alive in this situation was a genuine possibility.

"You made a good decision to find this hiding

spot near the humans," Buddy said. "Your parents will be very proud."

That made Kimba feel warm all over, but it was all very difficult to process. Buddy looked much better than the last time she had seen him weeks ago in Texas. Then, he appeared old and haggard and torn up. His nose was white from sunburns, and his eyes were dull. Now, he was young and fresh and bright-eyed and exactly like Commander Griffin, except for a few markings here and there. She sniffed at him, just to be sure.

Taking this as a welcome, Buddy rubbed his head against the top of hers. Such a familiar greeting was even more confusing for the lost white cat.

"We need to get you out of here," he said, locking eyes with her.

"How?"

"Trusted agents are monitoring two sets of mirrors here at the refuge."

Searching the area near them, Buddy determined where the restrooms and the break room were located. Both doorways were closed up tight.

"If we can get you inside that human building, and somehow get them to leave you alone, you can be easily transferred back to the ship and then to the safety of your human home."

"Is it really safe there?" she asked. "What about Hiro? Did they get her too?"

"Hiro is safe," he assured her, "and very worried about you. We are restricting all transfers, so no one can get their paws on her."

"Is Mama worried? She must have missed me by now."

"I'm sure, with morning coming, she will begin a frantic search. That's another good reason to get you back there soon."

The two cats watched from the tall grass as several humans in matching khaki outfits walked past, talking among themselves.

"The humans may be your best bet," he said. "They will probably take you inside somewhere, and then you can get closer to a mirror so those who are watching from the ship can find you."

"I was going to turn myself in to the humans this morning," she agreed. "I didn't know any other way to get to safety."

"Wise choice again," he said, blinking slowly.

She was certainly turning out to be more a part of the family than he had ever imagined when he had observed her as a kitten, he thought. She held potential for greatness and loyalty.

"You will make an excellent agent someday, Kimba. And who knows how far you can go after that."

How about high commander? she thought, flexing her claws.

A young woman dressed in khaki walked toward them. Buddy stood up tall.

"There," he said eagerly. "The female human is alone. Run to her now. Don't be shy or standoffish. Let her pick you up, and be as sweet as you can."

Kimba stared at him with wide eyes, and he bunted her with his head.

"Go. Run. Hurry!"

Obediently, Kimba leapt from the grassy area and ran straight for the young woman, stopping on the path directly in front of her.

"Meeeroow," she trilled meekly.

"Great heavens," the young woman said. "What are you doing here?"

Miss Fatty Cat's Revenge

Buddy was a wild and independent cat, but he was also loving and devoted.

Chapter 20
HELPFUL HUMANS

Kimba blinked at the bright lights of the break room. It smelled strange, like dirty work boots. She was grateful to be inside and safe, but she was also scared and hungry and simply wanted to go home. The young woman was more than happy to scoop her up and bring her to the break room the keepers and interns shared. She set the cat on the table in the middle of the room and started searching the cupboards for something to feed her.

"Poor little thing," she cooed, her head stuck in the refrigerator. "I don't know what we have for you to eat."

She shut the fridge and turned to look at Kimba

again. The white cat was hunkered in the middle of the table, staring at her.

"The big cats eat raw meat, but I don't imagine that would be very appealing to you."

She opened up other cabinets and sorted through them.

"Well, it's your lucky day, kitty," she said, pulling out a can of tuna and showing it to Kimba. "This should do the trick."

Kimba wasn't sure what was in the can, but she wasn't in the mood to be picky. Her tummy rumbled and grumbled as the woman opened up the can, dumped it onto a plate, and set it down in front of Kimba.

It smelled rather like the delicious fish Kimba and Hiro had eaten on their visit to the ship a few weeks ago, but something was not quite right about it either. On a normal day, Kimba would have turned her nose up at the tangy-smelling shreds. Today, she was too hungry to care. She slurped up several mouthfuls and gobbled them down.

A young man in a matching uniform entered the room and interrupted her breakfast.

"Hello there," he said. "What's a tiny kitty like you doing in a place like this?"

"She ran up to me this morning when I was headed to the front compound to feed the big cats. I was scared she might try to hide in one of the enclosures, so I brought her in here. Where do you suppose she came from?"

"The nearest houses are miles away," he said, "and she's too tidy to be a stray. She's not skinny either, so maybe she just got lost."

Both of the humans stared at Kimba, and she stared back, tuna juice dripping from her chin.

"I'll call over to Good Shepherd Humane Society later once they open up and see if anyone is looking for her," the young woman said. "Could she go home with you tonight if we can't find her owners? I already have six cats, and my roommate won't let me in the door with another one."

"Wish I could," he said, "but I don't know if I could keep her safe from all my dogs. Maybe she could just stay here for the night. We could set up a litter box in the corner for her. I'll call Cindy and ask her to bring some cat food and stuff from her house when she comes in this afternoon."

"Okay," she said. "She's safe enough in here for now. I've got some work to do on the computer, so I can keep her company."

Kimba eyed the mirror hanging next to the door. She hoped that whatever trusted cat was watching could see her and would be ready to transfer her as soon as she was left alone.

Special Agent Medusa Gloriosa couldn't believe her eyes.

"Felicity, I mean, High Commander, come here!" she called across the dark control room.

Everyone looked up, but no one moved from their stations as the high commander ran to Medusa's side. The fluffy cat tapped her computer monitor with her paw.

"That looks like her to me," she said.

She had been watching the break room at Turpentine Creek with the audio open, hoping for any clue about Kimba's whereabouts. Now there, sitting on the break room table as plain as day, was Kimba herself.

"Oh, she's alive." The high commander sighed.

"And it appears that she is safe for the time being," Medusa said.

"We have found her!" Felicity called out to the handful of cats in the huge room.

Cheers swirled in the air. At his transfer station, Snowball's heart rate slowed for the first time in hours. Kimba was alive. The High Council would relax, and finding Kimba safe and sound would keep the high commander from being quite so aggressive about finding the kidnapper.

"There's still a human in the room with her," Medusa said. "We can't risk the transfer."

"And we don't dare to do it if she is not expecting it," Felicity added. "She might think it is the rebels again and panic. We need to assure her that all is well first. Have you made contact with Buddy yet?" she called over to Artemis.

"No," he said. "It is too soon for his check-in, and the bathroom doors are shut. I am keeping watch, just in case."

"The minute Kimba is alone, open up that channel," the high commander said.

Medusa nodded her understanding. They were so close, but it wouldn't be over until Kimba was back where she belonged.

Felicity watched the monitor as the human

rummaged around in the cabinets for something to feed her daughter.

"Ugh, canned tuna," she said as she noticed the meal Kimba was served.

Medusa squinched her nose in silent agreement. Mummy would never have expected her to eat that.

Felicity had to admit that Kimba was doing well without any training at all, but it was time to start making plans for her future. Her daughter couldn't continue on Earth without some basic training. That much was clear.

"Medusa," the high commander said, "Kimba is going to need a mentor."

The two old friends locked eyes. Medusa narrowed her eyes and pursed her whiskers.

"I'm supposed to be retired from all of that now," she said.

"Are you refusing the honor of mentoring one of my daughters?" Felicity said, eyes wide but a playful twitch in her whiskers.

"Oh posh," Medusa said, flicking her ears in return, "don't pull rank like that."

"Kimba is going to need a firm and experienced paw to guide her in the right direction. Your stay on Earth should be complete about the same time that she is done with hers. I think it would be a perfect match."

"There's no point in refusing you, is there?"

"Hmmm," she purred, "refusing me has never worked for you before, has it?"

"No, my high commander, it has not," Medusa said, flicking her tail and blinking her blue eyes slowly.

"Then it's settled. Kimba may want to make other life-visits to Earth, but she's not going to return into another experience without some training. This abduction has proved that to be of the utmost importance."

"She got herself into the human room," Medusa said. "That shows amazing logical thinking."

"Or maybe Buddy got her there. We will find out soon enough. Look, the human is leaving," Felicity said, pointing her paw at the screen.

The two cats watched through the mirror as the young woman petted the top of Kimba's head and then walked out the main door. Kimba had finished eating her tuna and was taking a leisurely bath in the middle of the table. The moment the door shut she froze, her back leg stuck out at an odd angle, and she stared straight at the mirror.

"Greetings?" she said. "Is anyone there? The humans have all gone for the moment."

Medusa opened up the communication window. Her image and the high commander's appeared in the mirror. Kimba stood up tall on the table and breathed a very deep sigh.

"Greetings, Kimba. We are so glad to see you alive and well," her mother said. "This is Special Agent Medusa Gloriosa. She will continue this conversation while I go work out details for getting you out of there. Are you prepared to make a transfer?"

"Yes, ma'am," she said, "I am very ready."

"Good. We are going to bring you directly to the ship, and then we will find the right moment to return you to your human home. Stay where you are and be ready."

Kimba nodded and held very still. She could hear voices outside the door.

Hurry, Mother, she thought. *The humans could come back at any moment.*

The high commander raced for the transfer platform.

"Lock on to her," she yelled, leaping up to a station, "and bring her here."

"Prepare for the transfer," Commander Griffin ordered.

Snowball began to make the necessary adjustments for Kimba's location inside the concrete building. It was almost over. He just had to get her home safely, and then it would be forgotten.

At his small work station, Thoth froze, his paws hovering over the keyboard. There was no questioning what he saw on the screen. He had broken the code, and every moment of Kimba's unauthorized transfer was now right in front of him.

He peered over the top of his monitor at Snowball, just a few feet away. Thoth's ears lowered, and the fur along his spine rose.

"Traitor," he hissed. "Don't touch those keys!"

Chapter 21
THE PENALTY FOR TREASON

Every cat in the room turned to face Thoth. His eyes were wide and black with rage, ears laid flat. The swirls of orange-and-black fur on his back and tail rankled with his fury.

"Transfer Trainee Thoth," Commander Griffin said in his most firm voice, "this is no time for distractions. What are you talking about?"

Thoth rose from his station, his anger and intense loyalty to the Leaders of the ship fueling him on with courage he never knew he had. Snowball's ears twitched, and his bright-green eyes scanned the room for a means of escape.

"Traitor," Thoth hissed again, this time pointing a claw directly at Snowball.

All eyes turned to the longhaired white cat, his paws inches from the controls that governed Kimba's safety.

The high commander stared back at Thoth, her eyes narrowing.

"That is a fierce accusation, Trainee Thoth," she said, keeping a level tone.

Thoth's breath was coming in ragged gasps, and every hair on his body now stood on end.

"You did this," he growled at Snowball. "You made the transfer that put Kimba in the tiger's cage. It was YOU!"

"We need to get Kimba out of there now," Snowball said, looking around the room nervously. "This is our chance."

"Maybe you should step away from the controls," Medusa said, "until we can clear all of this up."

"There's no one else here who can perform the transfer," he argued. "The humans will be back soon, and she's waiting. The situation becomes increasingly dangerous every second!"

Kimba's parents locked eyes across the room, both knowing he was right.

"Trainee Thoth," the commander said. The

skinny tortie was so focused on Snowball that he didn't even hear. "THOTH!" Griffin yelled.

"Yes, sir," Thoth finally responded, coming to his senses.

"Get over there. Confirm Snowball's calculations."

Thoth raced to the control panel and double-checked everything.

"Snowball," the high commander said between clenched teeth, "I hope you understand that if anything happens to Kimba during this transfer, there will be nowhere in the universe for you to hide. I will lock you in the training rooms with coyotes and bobcats."

Her claws dug into the cushion of her seat as she contemplated what those wild animals would do to the fluffy white cat.

"Yes, High Commander," he gasped, "everything will be done correctly. I would never risk Kimba's safety."

"It looks good," Thoth admitted.

"Then bring my daughter here now," the high commander ordered.

Snowball watched the image of Kimba on the monitor. She was staring at the mirror, probably wondering what was taking so long. But she looked calm, so he tapped the final button. One bright flash of light, and Kimba disappeared from the table at the same time the break room door opened. The young woman stared at the spot where Kimba had just been.

"Kitty?" she whispered.

One, two, three, four, five, six . . . Kimba counted to herself, doing her best to remain calm. Before she reached seven, the hard surface of the transfer platform was under her paws. As the bright light faded, she saw her mother and father waiting for her at the base of the platform. There was a handful of other agents in the room, but it was quieter than her last visit.

"Oh, My Daughter," her mother said, racing up the steps to greet her. They rubbed heads in relief, and Felicity groomed Kimba's face with loving licks to comfort them both. The greeting was less formal than Kimba received the last time she was on the ship, and it was very welcome after such a long, scary night. Her mother stared into her eyes.

"Are you all right?" she asked.

"Yes," Kimba said. "Very tired and very confused, but I'm fine."

"That is to be expected, but we may have the answers for you soon. The humans are beginning to search for you. It would be best to return you to the family home on Earth as soon as possible. Regalus will tell us when the coast is clear."

"Regalus?" Kimba said, wondering if her ears were playing tricks on her. "What is he doing here?"

She had always imagined him off on some very unimportant job somewhere far away from headquarters. After his Facebook invasion plan had fallen apart, she had never heard from him again. Felicity pursed her whiskers, deciding how much to reveal to her young daughter.

"Special Agent Regalus is an honored member of my team, and he has always been loyal and done his part. I never blamed him for the failure of the Facebook plan. It was doomed from the start, and you know it was really just a test of how many cats would cooperate. When you went missing, Regalus was one of the first agents I turned to for help. Come and meet him."

Kimba and her mother climbed down from the

platform and wove their way through the empty computer stations to where the enormous gray cat was waiting for them.

"Greetings, Kimba," Regalus said.

"Greetings, Special Agent Regalus."

He was impressive in person, but not as fearsome as he had seemed through the mirror when she was only a kitten. His green eyes shifted back to the computer screen, and Kimba saw her sister sitting on her pillow outside the bathroom. Her back was twitchy, and she seemed nervous and anxious, but she was safe.

"Hiro will come talk to us when the humans are away. She is very worried about you and will be grateful to hear that you are secure and on the ship."

"Is it safe for me to go back to the house?" Kimba asked her mother. "I don't even know how I was transferred out."

"We do," the high commander said. "And some safeguards are being put in place to restrict any transfers in or out of your coordinate area. Once we are done, it will be the safest place in the universe for you and your sister."

Kimba heard arguing and hissing across the room, and the three of them turned to watch as the fluffy white cat with the bright-green eyes and flat face was led from the control room by two enormous orange Maine Coon cats.

"It wasn't me!" Snowball growled, trying to wiggle free.

"Wait," the high commander ordered, and everyone in the room froze. "Transfer Trainee Thoth, come here."

The skinny tortie trotted to her side.

"Are you positive that Senior Transfer Operations Specialist Snowball is responsible for the transfer that dropped Kimba at Turpentine Creek Wildlife Refuge?"

"Yes, High Commander. I'm positive. His passcode was entered to authorize it."

Kimba stared at Snowball, ears lowered and eyes wide. She hadn't expected to be face-to-face with the rebel cat so soon. He didn't seem dangerous, but he had put her through an experience she would never forget. Not in hundreds of years.

What a waste, Felicity thought. *All those decades of training and support, and this is how he repays us.*

"Someone could have stolen my code!" Snowball argued. "There's no proof I had anything to do with Kimba's transfer."

"Commander Griffin," Felicity said, "you have studied the evidence. Do you agree with Trainee Thoth that Snowball's code was used for the transfer?"

He nodded stiffly in agreement, and Felicity knew from the glare in his eyes that her mate was inches away from taking justice into his own paws. He could dispatch Snowball in a few seconds, but that was not the proper way to handle this. Her rank demanded that she follow protocol and not allow either of their emotions to get the best of them. Her ears twitched and swiveled in thought.

A trial through the High Council was the next logical step, but that could take months. So few cats ever got in trouble. The elders would need a refresher course on the rules of law before they even began to decide Snowball's fate. But what if she could handle it all right now? A risky plan formed in her mind. It was worth a try.

"And do you suppose, Commander Griffin," she continued confidently, "that when we check the records from the security video cameras around the transfer terminals that we will gain the positive proof necessary to convict Snowball of this crime?"

"Cameras?" Snowball growled. "What cameras?"

The high commander tipped her head and glared at him.

"You don't suppose that areas on the ship as important as the transfer platforms are unsupervised, do you?"

Snowball lowered his ears and crouched down between the two guard cats.

"Senior Transfer Operations Specialist Snowball, maybe we can make a deal instead of wasting so much time on evidence and trials."

Snowball narrowed his eyes, but he nodded his head for her to continue.

"I have already spoken with Horus and doubt she will give you any support. She will say you acted alone, and you will say the same thing to protect the League For Cat Equality. That is all very bothersome. I know how things work, and I won't believe either of you. What I also know is that you will take the blame for attempted murder of the daughter of the high commander. This is a very serious charge. Do you understand?"

"But she is alive and safe, and everything is fine now," he said.

"True," she agreed, twitching her whiskers, "but you never know how the High Council will see it.

Your trial would be a perfect opportunity to make an example of one of the rebels. We could throw the book at you, as the humans say. It could be very messy, or..."

"Or?" Snowball said.

"You can agree to an immediate and appropriate punishment right now. No High Council. No trial. No other cats involved but those of us in this room."

"I think that would be best," Commander Griffin said, nodding at his mate.

He wasn't exactly sure what she was up to, but he suspected she had a plan. There was always a chance that the old ones on the High Council might decide not to bother with a trial since Kimba was safe. He wanted justice, and he wanted it *now*.

"What punishment?" Snowball asked, eyes wide.

"You and your League For Cat Equality seem very attached to the human legal system. They have a phrase: Let the punishment fit the crime."

Griffin winked at her, and Snowball's eyes darted around the room. He found no support from any of the loyal agents there. Thoth snorted in anger, and Medusa pursed her whiskers in complete disdain for such awful behavior.

"My Daughter," Felicity said, turning to Kimba,

"what do you think is a fitting consequence for the actions taken against you over the last few hours of your young life?"

Kimba's eyes narrowed as she faced the cat responsible for trying to kill her. Her tail thrashed as she thought of the horrible things she would like to see happen to him.

Let the punishment fit the crime, she thought.

"I suppose," she said, "that he should have to go through exactly what I went through."

"Ah," Felicity said, her ears perking up. "An excellent idea. Trainee Thoth, enter the exact coordinates for Kimba's original transfer into the refuge."

"What?" Snowball gasped. "I don't have any training for that kind of situation. I'm not an agent. I'm just a transfer technician!"

The high commander curled her tail around her feet in satisfaction.

"It is true that you are not a trained agent, but neither is Kimba. She is a brand-new cat, only two years old. You have hundreds of years of experience. You believed she could survive it, so you must be able to as well. I mean, you did expect her to survive, didn't you? Otherwise, we should begin a conversation about very serious charges."

"Yes, of course I expected her to survive." Snowball sighed in defeat.

To admit he hadn't much cared whether she lived through her meeting with the big cat would have thrown him into a whole new pile of dirty litter. He imagined he stood a better chance against the tiger than against the enraged High Council.

Felicity nodded to the security guards, and Snowball was led onto the transfer platform, where he hunkered down in fear.

"Snowball," the high commander proclaimed, "you are hereby sentenced to twenty-four hours on the Earth's surface in the exact location where you sent Kimba. Special Agent Artemis will continue to monitor the bathroom mirrors at the refuge. If you can survive and make contact, we will retrieve you, and that will be the end of your punishment. I'm sure we can find something useful for you to do here on the ship when you return. There are always floors or toilets in need of cleaning. Do you understand this arrangement and agree to it in front of these witnesses?"

"I do," Snowball growled, "but you can't stop progress from happening. The League For Cat

Equality will be heard. You cannot silence them forever!"

"Maybe not," she agreed, "but they must learn that there is a right and honest way to accomplish their goals. Kidnapping my children is not one of them."

"Remember to relax, Snowball," Thoth said with a snarl. "Things can go very wrong if you fight it or panic."

Thoth didn't mind the idea of something going wrong, but he didn't want it to happen when he was at the controls. Commander Griffin was supervising the process, and he would rather impress the important cat than get rid of the traitor. Thoth was pretty sure there would be some promotions available in the transfer department once Snowball was out of the way.

"Beginning in ten seconds," Thoth warned.

Snowball nodded, eyes wide and tail puffed. Preparing others for a transfer was very different from experiencing it himself. A tickling sensation crept along his spine.

"Snowball," Kimba added, "say hello to Karma's brother for me."

Chapter 22
MEDUSA AND KIMBA

Once Snowball was delivered, the atmosphere at headquarters relaxed. Regalus and Artemis continued to monitor their mirrors. A replacement transfer operations specialist was called in to prepare for Medusa and Kimba's return trips to Earth. While they waited, Thoth and Griffin had a lengthy discussion about the technical rules of the transfer process.

Felicity ordered some snacks from the mess hall for Kimba and Medusa before their journeys. The three of them gathered on pillows near the transfer platform, and the high commander introduced her youngest daughter to her oldest friend.

"My Daughter," she said, "this is my most trusted friend, Special Agent Medusa Gloriosa."

"Greetings," Kimba said formally.

She thought Medusa had the most amazing blue eyes she had ever seen. They were even bluer than the Siamese Artemis.

"Greetings, Kimba," Medusa said with a twitch of her whiskers. "Your mother wants us to begin working together on your training as an agent."

"An agent?" Kimba asked. "Right now?"

"No, no, well, not like you think," Medusa said. "We can begin some communications and training soon, but mostly it will be after you and I are both done with our current Earth placements."

"Oh," Kimba said, grateful they didn't expect her to remain on the ship just yet.

"We will arrange group communications between the two of you and Artemis while you are both on Earth," her mother added. "Medusa can begin the very basics of your training and help you learn what you can while you are still on the planet."

The snacks arrived, and each of the cats enjoyed the tender bits of fresh fish. With a full tummy to start, Kimba and Medusa shouldn't be desperate for food when they arrived on Earth.

It's much better than canned tuna, Kimba thought, licking a piece of salmon with her rough tongue before she gobbled it down.

Medusa and Kimba's eyes met over their snacks, and Medusa winked at her. Kimba sensed that this was the start of a long and vital relationship in her life. Her mother's most trusted special agent was going to teach her how to be an agent. Kimba was delighted and blinked her eyes slowly in return.

"Training is a good idea," Kimba said. "I want to be ready the next time some rebels snatch me off the sofa while I'm asleep."

"Off the sofa?" her mother said. "Do you mean you were not in front of a mirror when you were transferred?"

"No, ma'am," she said. "There are no mirrors in the basement game room. I fell asleep on the sofa there and woke up in the liger cage."

Medusa and Felicity exchanged worried looks.

"What's wrong?" Kimba asked.

"That means there were more cats involved. Possibly someone in the house with you," Medusa said. "Snowball wouldn't have been able to find you otherwise. I mean, it can be done, but it is a very tricky business. I suppose, if he knew where the house was located before we did, he could have scanned for your fur and found you."

"That must be it. Who else would it be? I can't imagine Agent Ebony getting involved in this mess," the high commander said. "She would have no reason to side with the League For Cat Equality. Anything that requires that much effort is not really her style."

"Who is Agent Ebony?" Kimba asked.

"Your humans call her Miss Fatty Cat," the high commander said. "She and her sister are both visiting Earth from the ship."

"Wow," Kimba said, ears flushing pink. "She told me she didn't know anything about any Cats in the Mirror or special missions. Why would she lie about that?"

"Mostly because she wants nothing to do with us while she is on Earth. No missions, just a vacation. As I said, I can't believe she would get mixed up in the League's nonsense. I still can't believe that my agents hidden inside the League didn't know anything about your being transferred. Whether Agent Ebony was involved, or whether it was just Snowball acting on his own, it's all a very strange business."

"We will need to remain careful and alert,"

Medusa said. "That is your first lesson, Kimba. Strange things happen on Earth all the time. You should never get too comfortable."

Kimba nodded. That was a good first lesson.

"We have eyes on Buddy," Artemis called out. "He has made it into the bathroom and has given an indication that he is ready."

"Excellent," the high commander said. "Don't bother with opening a channel, just get him back here now."

Poof, a flash of light, and Buddy appeared on the platform. Without pause, he trotted to meet with Felicity and Kimba.

"From what I heard the humans say about a vanishing cat, it was pretty clear that you had been recovered," he said. "I am glad to see that it is true. No worse for wear?"

"No, I'm fine, thank you, Buddy. I'm really grateful that you risked coming to rescue me."

"It is my duty and my honor," he said, ears alert. "But let's not do it again anytime soon."

"Agreed."

"Medusa," Commander Griffin said, "another senior transfer operations specialist has arrived, and the site is clear for you to return to your Earth home. Your double says the human is still at work."

"I hope Mummy didn't miss me much. She is a very devoted human," she added with a twitch of her whiskers. "There is nothing more wonderful than an Earth placement in a loving human home."

Kimba nodded in agreement. Living on the ship and being an agent would be great one day, but today all she wanted was to be home with her sister.

Chapter 23
HOME AGAIN

Hiro woke to find the house was quiet. She had tried desperately to stay awake, but sooner or later a cat must sleep. She jumped down from her bed and checked for humans. The house was empty. Racing back to the bathroom, Hiro leapt onto the counter and put both front paws on the mirror.

"Greetings! Hello? The coast is clear. Do you have Kimba?"

Regalus opened the communication channel, and Hiro was faced with the dark-gray cat again.

"Greetings, Hiro," Regalus said. "We noticed you wake up and were listening for your update. Kimba is here. She is safe and is preparing to come home. We will transfer her to your bed, directly behind you. Then we will have visual confirmation of her safe arrival."

"Finally." Hiro sighed in relief.

"Stand by," Regalus said.

A moment later, a flash of light reflected in the mirror, and Hiro's sister appeared. She stood on the pillow for a moment, then she flopped down with a groan.

"Oh, it's good to be home."

Hiro rushed to her side, and the sisters greeted each other with rubs and head bunts and kisses.

"I thought I'd never see you again." Hiro purred, rubbing the top of her head against her sister's.

"Me too, but wait until you hear about what happened to me. I met a grizzly bear," Kimba whispered.

"A grizzly bear?"

"And a liger."

"What's a liger?" Hiro said, eyes wide.

"My Daughters," the high commander called from the mirror, "if all is well, we will leave you alone for now."

Kimba had not realized they were still watching.

A bit embarrassed, she sat up and licked at her fur once or twice.

"I'm fine," Kimba assured her. "Thank you, all of you, for getting me back home safely."

The high commander nodded goodbye, and the Cats in the Mirror vanished. Nothing remained but Kimba's very rumpled-looking image.

"Tell me about the bear," Hiro whispered.

KIMBA HAD JUST GOTTEN to the part of the story where Buddy found her at the refuge when she heard Mama's voice in the hallway.

"It just doesn't make any sense," Mama said, her voice tinged with worry. "How could she possibly have gotten outside?"

"I don't know," Daddy said, following her into the bedroom, "but she just isn't anywhere in the house."

They both froze at the sight of Kimba and Hiro curled up on the pillow together.

"You have got to be kidding me," Mama said, putting her hand on her hips in exasperation.

Kimba gazed back at her and blinked. Hiro licked

the top of her sister's head twice and pursed her whiskers at Daddy.

"Where have you been, Kimba Baby?" Mama cooed, kneeling down next to the cedar chest and Hiro's bed. "I have been looking all over for you."

Sorry to have worried you, Mama, she thought, *but it wasn't my fault.*

"Well, you are just fine. One blue eye and one green eye, just as it should be."

She allowed Mama to pet her and fuss over her until the woman finally wandered away to open more boxes.

Watching as Mama left the bedroom, Kimba saw Miss Fatty Cat peeking in. The moment she noticed Kimba looking her way, she darted back under Leia's bed.

What if the high commander was right and someone inside the house helped Snowball find me? She had to agree that it would take a lot of effort for the lazy Miss Fatty Cat to get involved with the rebels, but Kimba would keep her eyes and ears open from now on.

"Hiro," she whispered, "has Miss Fatty Cat been acting weird while I was gone?"

"Yesss," she whispered back, "totally weird."

"Mother says that she is an agent. She knows all about the Cats in the Mirror."

"I know. She admitted it," Hiro said, sitting up and glaring out the doorway.

"Mother thinks that maybe she had something to do with the rebels capturing me. Maybe she even helped them find me in the house. But there's no way to prove it."

"Oooo," Hiro growled, "I knew it, but she totally denied knowing anything."

"Mother says we are super-safe for now. They have put in all kinds of extra security, but I think we should be careful anyhow. Don't trust Miss Fatty Cat."

"I never did," Hiro said. "Just let her try to thawunk me. That lying fat cat has a surprise coming her way."

"Fatty Cat?" Agent Ebony heard Leia calling her when she came in the room, shutting the door behind her. A moment later the girl's face peeked under the bed. "There you are, silly girl. Come on out."

Grabbing Miss Fatty Cat by the back legs, Leia dragged her out into the open. The cat tried to resist, but on the new slick wood floors there was nothing for her claws to grab onto. She found herself sprawled out on the bedroom floor with nowhere else to run.

"Hew-wo, my sweet baby kitty," Leia cooed, scooping the fat cat up into her arms. "Oh, you are so soft and squishy-wishy."

Miss Fatty Cat braced herself for the indignities to come, but then Hiro's words echoed in her thoughts. Was this just Leia's way of spoiling her?

The girl nuzzled her face into the cat's soft black fur and gave her kisses all over the top of her head. Climbing up onto the bed with the cat clutched in her arms, Leia grabbed a blanket and wrapped Miss Fatty Cat up tight.

"You can help me get my summer reading done today," she whispered, tucking the swaddled cat under her arm. "We have to find out if Lucy can save Mr. Tumnus."

Miss Fatty Cat had learned not to fight it when Leia was determined to cuddle, but this time she tried to think of it in a different way altogether. The girl wasn't trying to be mean. She simply wanted company.

Does she lock me in her room with her because she loves me? Miss Fatty Cat wondered.

Her yellow-orange eyes stared up at the girl, and Leia gazed at her with adoration. A purr rumbled up from deep in Miss Fatty Cat's throat.

Being loved is good, I suppose, she thought. *Even if it means being wrapped up like a baby.*

Miss Fatty Cat closed her eyes and felt Leia's warmth coming through the blankets. It wasn't such a bad way to get a nap after all.

Miss Fatty Cat loved her time on Leia's bed.

Chapter 24
OPERATION OZARK OCCUPATION

Felicity sat watching through the mirror long after the communication channel was closed. Her daughters groomed each other and spoke in low voices that she couldn't hear. They were content.

"Commander Griffin," she said, "see to it immediately that security cameras are installed in the transfer areas."

Griffin twitched his ears and nodded. Felicity flexed her whiskers back at him.

"Well, it worked didn't it?" she said.

"A well-played deception," he agreed. "Do you suppose Snowball will make it to his retrieval point?"

"I almost hope he doesn't," she admitted, "but

his disappearance would be difficult to explain. It's probably best that he makes it back and lives to tell the story of his complete and utter failure. The League may deny knowing what he was up to, but I don't believe Horus for one minute. They should think twice before they do something so outrageous again."

"His punishment got me thinking," Griffin said. "The ships are getting crowded, and the cats are becoming antsy. Whether or not we have the support from Earth cats, it really is time for another large group transfer."

Regalus cleared his throat and shifted in his seat.

"Would you want to run the operation?" Griffin asked him.

"I'm not sure," Regalus said. "I thought I was put in charge of an invasion before, but it turned out to be nothing. No cat should be forced to spend that amount of time on Facebook only to find out it is just a test for new agents."

The high commander tipped her head in sympathy.

"I understand," she said, "but this time would be different. This time would be real."

"You know you can count on me to follow whatever orders you issue," Regalus said. "I will always obey."

"It would be best if we don't mention anything about this to Kimba and Hiro," she said. "All of their experiences with humans have been wonderful. They have not seen the things we have. I lived through the Salem Witch Trial massacres. We have all read the historical documents. Some humans are good. Some are monsters. I have no problem sending a group of brave cats to Earth to try and forge a place for themselves there. One day the humans will all manage to kill each other off, and I won't be terribly sorry to see them go. As long as they leave the planet mostly intact, we can take over for good."

"There seems to be a lot of wooded, unsettled areas around that Turpentine Creek place," Griffin suggested. "Surveys indicate caves and weather that is not too extreme."

"So should I begin to work on plans?" Regalus asked.

Griffin and Felicity exchanged questioning looks and knew the other's thoughts without words being spoken. That happens after over two hundred years together.

"Begin preparations, Special Agent Regalus," she said. "And include as many of those rebels as you can."

Don't miss Book 4 in the Cats in the Mirror Series!
Keep reading for a sample of Chapter 1.

Slinky Steps Out, Chapter 1
MOVING BOXES

Slinky watched in horror as Mindy pulled the clear packing tape across the top of yet another big cardboard box. The piercing sound of the tape was bad enough, but the reality of what packed boxes meant was even worse.

They were moving. Again.

"Should we take Mufasa?" the girl asked her cat, wrapping her arms around the giant stuffed toy. "It seems a shame to leave him behind."

"You wanted to take him on trips with us when you were little," Mama said as she wandered into the room.

She set a basket of clean laundry down on the bed, careful to stay just far enough away from Slinky not to startle her. It was easy to startle Slinky, and her eyes were wide today.

"I remember wanting to take him." Mindy smiled. "I pretended that Mufasa was running along the ground under the airplane so he could be in Florida with us at Grandpa's house."

Mama nodded and picked a book from the shelf.

"Are you going to leave most of these here?" she asked.

"I think so. I can always come get them if I need them, but I think the assignments will keep me busy enough."

"Okay." Mama shrugged. "Dinner's almost ready."

She started to leave, but then she hesitated in the doorway.

"Are you really sure you want to take Slinky with you? I know it's allowed in the apartment, but I'm just worried that she will be scared and lonely with you gone so much of the day."

Mindy set the packing tape down. Both of them looked at Slinky, crouching nervously on the bed. She stared back at them with bright-yellow eyes.

"Don't you think she'd miss me even more if I left her here?"

"I suppose so." Mama nodded and headed upstairs to finish making dinner.

"What do you think, Slinks?" Mindy said. "Are you ready for college?"

Slinky blinked twice, but she didn't know what to say. She didn't know what college was. But she did know that she didn't want Mindy to go anywhere without her. She hopped up on a nearby box and meowed sweetly. Her girl scratched the top of her head and right behind her ears.

"I'm not sure I'm ready either," Mindy admitted. "But we can face it together."

From on top of a box in the game room, Kimba twitched her ears.

College? What's college? she wondered. Whatever it was, there were moving boxes involved. Headquarters needed to know about it.

THAT AFTERNOON, when the house was empty of humans, Kimba hopped up on the bathroom sink in her usual place. She stared into the mirror expectantly.

"Greetings," she said.

For a moment, there was silence, and then an image crackled in the mirror and Special Agent Artemis, her old friend, appeared.

"Greetings, Kimba," he said, wiping a paw across his mouth. "Excuse me. You caught me at breakfast."

"My apologies," she said but knew it wasn't really necessary. Agents answered calls at every hour of the day and night without complaint. It was part of the job.

"Is something wrong?" Artemis asked.

"I'm not sure," she admitted. "They are packing boxes downstairs."

"Is the family moving again?" he asked, suddenly more alert and expectant.

"I don't think so. No one else is packing anywhere else. Just Mindy. I listened in from the game room and heard her talking to Mama about 'college.' Do you know what that is?"

Artemis relaxed and sat back in his seat.

"Ah, yes. College. It is like the advanced training we receive here on the ship."

"Is it dangerous?"

"No, no," he laughed, "not at all. Mindy will continue her schooling away from home. That is all. She is entering the adult human experience."

"I see," Kimba said, still not quite sure.

"Did they say where she would be living? In a dorm room, perhaps?"

"No, they called it an apartment. And it sounds like Slinky is going with her."

That bit of information got his attention, and he began to rapidly click around on his computer.

"Agent Onyx, yes," he said, still looking off at another part of the screen. "I had quite forgotten she was in the house with you."

"That's easy to do. All she does is hide in Mindy's room."

"Well, she is a timid soul," he admitted. "The high commander was hesitant to send her to Earth at all, but her work as an agent had to begin sometime. Going with her sister seemed a good fit. Does Agent Ebony, your Miss Fatty Cat, know about this development?"

"I don't think so. I wanted to talk with you first and find out what was really going on."

"I will advise the High Command of this possible transfer of location. You need to let Agent Ebony know. They are not actually littermates, like they are on Earth. Ebony is about a hundred years older than Onyx, but she takes diligent care of her little sister.

Ebony will be able to remind her about how to mark the mirrors and help us find her again after the move. Losing track of her is out of the question. Their parents are important special agents and are on the High Council."

Artemis clicked some more keys on the computer, but he didn't seem to be getting the answers he desired.

"Is there a mirror in Mindy's bedroom?" he asked.

"I don't know. I'm sure there's one in her bathroom downstairs."

"Good. We will do a search and tune in immediately to begin monitoring the situation. Keep your ears open. Listen for when they are leaving and details about where they are going. That will help us narrow down the search. And talk to Agent Ebony immediately. If boxes are being packed, the move must be soon. She needs to help her sister prepare."

"Understood." Kimba nodded and pursed her whiskers.

She didn't look forward to interacting with Miss Fatty Cat, but she knew it was important to keep track of Slinky. If the ship lost contact with her, they would never be able to bring her back at the end of her Earth-life. Kimba wanted no part of an agent being lost forever. It was unthinkable.

"Let me know if there are any other major developments," Artemis said. "I will keep the audio on this mirror open so we can hear you, even if we cannot respond because humans are around."

Kimba nodded again, feeling the fur rise up along her spine. Not much ever happened around her Earth house, but this was big. Life-changing big. She would not blow it.

End of Chapter 1 Sample

Don't miss out on the rest of the
Cats in the Mirror Series!

And the Companion Books to the Series

Also by Meg Welch Dendler

"Princess Bianca rules, in every way!"
New England Children's Book Review

Best Juvenile Book 2018
Oklahoma Writers' Federation

BIANCA
Journey to Ryuugito

Meg Welch Dendler

And For Older Readers

Penny had been stuck in the same cozy diner for decades—ever since she died in 1952. Then ridiculously handsome bad boy biker Jake dropped in and became stuck as well, turning her world upside down. Should Penny risk losing it all for a chance at love?

Being part tiger and part human should be an advantage—not lead to extermination. Young tigran Taliya has been forced to flee her home. Paired with a male white tigran named Kano, Taliya is determined to survive, but what awaits her is more challenging than she ever imagined.

If you enjoyed Miss Fatty Cat's story, please take a moment to leave a review at your favorite store and tell your friends!

Sign up for Meg's Readers' Group
(at megdendler.com)
to hear about new books, sales, and other exciting events in the lives of Kimba and her friends.

Author's Note

As with the other books in the series, this book follows some real events in Kimba and Hiro's lives. We did move the family to Arkansas, and all four cats came with us.

You can find videos of Kimba stealing my Disney toys and singing about it at my YouTube channel.

Kimba thought every day of packing and playing on boxes was one giant party.

Our dear cat Buddy did pass on at a ripe old age, but it was actually two years before that move. He was lost in the woods when we found him at about a year old, and he was lost again in Houston for eighteen months. I've always wished he could talk and tell me his stories. Now I love to think of him as being off on another grand adventure. I have big plans for Buddy in later books, so you haven't heard the last of him yet.

Buddy, in the last year of his Earth-life.

Turpentine Creek Wildlife Refuge is a real place (you can find information about them at the end of the book). It was a short drive from our home, and I fell in love with everything about it from my first visit. My blog is full of stories of volunteering there and helping to build new enclosures on Rescue Ridge. There were two cats living in the offices there: a stray with an odd tail named Crook and a bengal cat mix named Sabena. I didn't know about them yet when I wrote this book or I would have definitely included them.

Crook the office cat, helping me file at Turpentine Creek Wildlife Refuge.

Leia and I helped build Bam Bam the grizzly bear's new large enclosure, and I freely admit to adoring both Karma and Brady the ligers. If you have never heard a lion caroling, go to the refuge at feeding time. It is an amazing sound. Thank you to Ivy for helping me check my facts and to Kyle for providing photos.

There are a few new cat friends joining us in this book. Transfer Trainee Thoth is a creation of my imagination, but Special Agent Medusa Gloriosa is based on a real cat. Her owner loves to post photos of her on Facebook, and I fell in love with the beautiful Medusa. I knew she would make a great character, and as her alter ego/alien cat personality unfolded, her place in the story became clear. You can expect to hear a lot more from Medusa in the series.

I have plans for more books in the Cats in the Mirror series. There are so many stories to tell, and with transfer technology, the cats can go anywhere in the world. I hope you will continue on the adventures with me to discover what lies ahead for Kimba and Hiro and all of my wonderful characters.

Medusa, lounging at home with her mummy.

Gratitude

Many thanks go to my husband for constantly encouraging and supporting this publishing adventure. He deals with the cheerleading and bookkeeping so I can focus on the stories and sharing them with you.

And I'm immensely grateful to Kelsey Rice for helping me get the covers ready for this second edition. It is important to have folks on your team whom you can trust and who possess the skills you do not. Kelsey always makes my covers shine.

And a huge thank you to each of you for reading my Cats in the Mirror series!

Thank you!!

Photo that was used for the cover design. Miss Fatty Cat, on her favorite sofa. As grown-up cats, she and Kimba and Hiro got along just fine.

Words You May Not Know

The teacher in me loves to throw fun words into my stories, but you may find that some of them are new to you. Here's a few from each chapter, just in case you need to check on what they mean in the story.

Chapter 1

stealthy: (adj.) slow, deliberate, and intended to be secret and go unnoticed

hurrah: (interjection) used as a cheer, praise, congratulations, and encouragement

lugging: (verb) dragging, pulling, or carrying with great effort

Chapter 2

suffocatingly: (adv.) involving smothering, inability to breathe, and a lack of fresh air

Piglet: (noun) character from the stories of Winnie the Pooh; Pooh Bear's best friend

Ovaltine: (noun) chocolate malt mix that is added to milk

sauntered: (verb) walked in a slow or leisurely manner; rambled or strolled

valiantly: (adv.) bravely, with great courage and effort, or heroically

bitter: (adj.) very acrid, harsh, or unpleasant

groggy: (verb) weak or unsteady; dazed, sleepy, or extremely tired

Chapter 3

agitated: (adj.) disturbed, upset, or mentally troubled

registration: (noun) recorded list of names, facts, etc. about an individual

bustling: (verb) to act with a lot of energy and move around quickly with purpose

"taken down a peg or two": (idiom) to scold someone who is acting too boldly or arrogantly; to damage someone's ego or pride; to humble someone and get them to behave

newbies: (noun) individuals who are brand-new or inexperienced

protocol: (noun) customs, rules, and etiquette in dealing with important individuals or dignitaries

Chapter 4

Himalayan: (noun) breed of cats that is a cross

between a Siamese and a Persian, with a long coat of cream and brown and blue eyes

"Best in Show": (noun) top award/title earned by the best of the best in all of the categories at a show

immaculately: (adv.) spotlessly cleaned and tidy; done without flaw or error

glamorous: (adj.) combination of charm and good looks that make someone exciting and attractive; having an almost magical quality of beauty

indignity: (noun) injury to a person's dignity; insult, dishonor, or humiliation

imperative: (adj.) absolutely necessary, required, or unavoidable

Chapter 5

chaos: (noun) a state of total confusion and disorder

teetered: (verb) moved unsteadily or with lack of balance

callumped: (verb) falling down or landing in a clumsy way with a loud thump—word made up by the author

squander: (verb) waste foolishly or needlessly

"bargaining tool": (idiom) something that can be used to your advantage or to get what you want when making a deal or agreement

banished: (verb) sent away, removed, or exiled from home or any specific area, usually by a formal decree or law

harsh: (adj.) grim, stern, cruel, uncomfortable, or unpleasant

Chapter 6

sector: (noun) area or specific part of a larger whole, in this case a small portion of the whole ship

lumbered: (verb) moved clumsily or heavily, usually because of weight, like an elephant

nonchalantly: (adv.) coolly unconcerned, not worried, or using extra effort to appear calm and casual

noble: (adj.) of high moral character or excellence; of high quality or superiority

Chapter 7

gargantuan: (adj.) massive beyond belief; more than just gigantic

enclosure: (noun) area that is fenced off or sectioned off in some way to hold creatures inside of it; nicer term for what is basically a very large cage

tentatively: (adv.) hesitantly, unsurely, or questionably

"push her luck": (idiom) taking a risk but counting on good luck to continue and the results to be positive or in your favor

slunk: (verb) move in a fearful, slow, or hesitant way, usually low to the ground

chuffed: (verb) gentle, reassuring, friendly noise made by tigers that sounds like a puff of breath

Chapter 8

prime: (adj.) first in rank, value, or significance

assassinated: (verb) to kill someone suddenly or in secret, usually someone who is important, high-ranking, or of political importance

maintenance: (noun) the care, upkeep, repairs, and maintaining of equipment or structures, like a spaceship

Chapter 9

chow: (noun) a slang word for food or a meal

flailed: (verb) moved, swung, or beat wildly; thrashed about

feline: (adj.) cat-like

Words You May Not Know

foraging: (verb) digging, hunting, rummaging, or searching about for something, usually food

chortled: (verb) laughed deeply; chuckled

tinge: (noun) a slight trace of something

forlorn: (adj.) sad, sorrowful, dreary, or unhappy

Chapter 10

roused: (verb) woke up or was awoken from sleep or a dazed state

skitter: (verb) to run or move quickly but in a jittery, inconsistent, or jerky way

clenched: (verb) closed tightly, like a fist; gripped firmly and securely

Chapter 11

inconvenienced: (verb) made trouble for, interfered with, upset, or disturbed

antsy: (adj.) uneasy, nervous, unable to sit still, or fidgety

coordinates: (noun) a set of numbers used to find the location something in time and space

indefinitely: (adv.) for a length of time that has not been determined, is vague, or is unsure and could last forever

malfunction: (noun) failure to work or operate in the correct or expected way

mole: (noun) hidden spy; double agent; individual who claims to support one side but is really gathering information for another; spy who is undercover or "underground," like a mole

Chapter 12

ominously: (adv.) threateningly, causing fear or suggesting something bad will happen; menacingly

cinder block: (noun) a hollow block used for building, made from coal and cement cinders or ashes

pressurized: (adj.) to create a great pressure inside a container that allows the substance to be shot forth with great speed and force, in this case a great blast of water

wheezing: (adj.) a sound someone makes when breathing with great difficulty or a whistling noise, like when one has a chest cold

Chapter 13

surveyed: (verb) took in the general situation by looking around and gathering details to make a decision

frantic: (adj.) desperate or wild with excitement, fear, or some other large emotion

trepidation: (noun) fear, alarm, trembling, or uncertainty

double: (noun) an individual who looks enough like someone else that they could pretend to be each other, like a twin but not actually related

rogue: (adj.) dangerous, uncontrollable, rebellious, or disobedient

Chapter 14

in route: (verb) on the way or following the most direct path to arrive somewhere

determination: (noun) fixed and unyielding effort to reach a goal; firmness of purpose and intention

personnel: (noun) employees or workers, in this case agents

reprimand: (noun) scolding, yelling at, or criticism

compromised: (verb) revealed or exposed, especially of a spy or mole, instead of remaining hidden or secret

rallying: (verb) gathering together for a common purpose; coming together for a common goal

rout: (verb) win, beat, or conquer someone or something completely; defeat without question

disavow: (verb) disown or claim to have absolutely no knowledge of something or someone; refuse to acknowledge or accept

pelt: (noun) skin or more specifically animal skin with fur; used in the book more as the idiom "save your own skin" or worry about your own safety

Chapter 15

abduction: (noun) carry off a person without their consent; kidnapping

majestically: (adv.) splendidly, royally, grandly, or beautifully

abandon: (verb) desert; leave behind completely and totally; take away support, protection, or help

squinched: (verb) contorted the features, squeezed together and contracted, or squinted

coyly: (adv.) shyly and modestly, though usually just pretending to be that way; marked by cute and tactful playfulness

Chapter 16

negotiate: (verb) deal or make a bargain before making a deal; discussion before coming to terms on some issue

plagued: (verb) annoyed, worried, and tormented

fretted: (verb) expressed worry, discontent, annoyance, or fear

lurched: (verb) moved with an awkward swaying motion; staggered

domain: (noun) territory or land that belongs to an individual

agitated: (adj.) excited or disturbed

Chapter 17

doted on: (verb) lavished with extra attention, love, and adoration; cherished and praised excessively

pouted: (verb) moody and silently expressed unhappiness; sulked, moped, or glowered

"walls might have ears": (idiom) the room or walls might have listening devices installed for spying on conversations or others could be listening in on a conversation

persuasion: (noun) attempting to influence someone, convince them, or change their mind or behavior

warily: (adv.) cautiously or carefully, watchful and worried about danger

hostage: (noun) someone held prisoner or captive, usually for a short time until another individual gives you what you want

consequences: (noun) outcome, effect, or results of some earlier action, often bad or unhappy

Chapter 18

coded: (verb) wrote a specific computer code or

system of numbers a computer would recognize, in this case a secret one

remains: (noun) what is left behind after someone has died; dead body or parts of it

"in earnest": (idiom) with purposeful and sincere intent and effort; trying really hard and being focused

"card to play": (idiom) last chance or idea, like having one more card in your hand during a game and having a bit of hope that you still can win

blatant: (adj.) obviously offensive or designed to be rude

oppression: (noun) unjust or cruel use of power and authority to keep others down; tyranny

prevail: (verb) to win, overcome, or be successful

traitor: (noun) someone who betrays or turns against their country, government, or another person they are supposed to support and be loyal to; turncoat or double-crosser

Chapter 19

flinching: (verb) moving or looking away from; recoiling, or cringing, expecting something bad to happen

intrusion: (noun) taking or going into someone else's space, property, or territory without permission or invitation; trespass

grave: (adj.) serious, somber, vital, or deathly important

gravelly: (adv.) harsh, rough, or grating, like it is coming through or has been roughed up by gravel or rocks

haggard: (adj.) wild or wild-looking, exhausted, hollow-eyed, or extremely tired-looking

khaki: (adj.) dull yellowish-brown color, often associated with uniforms in the military and at zoos

standoffish: (adj.) cold, distant, or unfriendly

Chapter 20

tangy: (adj.) strong, pungent, sharp flavor or smell, usually not in a good way

tidy: (adj.) clean, neat, and well cared for

rummaged: (verb) searched through completely and thoroughly, usually involving moving things around, looking through them, and excessive activity

mentor: (noun) wise, experienced, and trusted teacher, counselor, or advisor

posh: (interjection) used as an exclamation of disgust or disregard, like "how silly" or "don't be ridiculous"

"pull rank": (idiom) to make use of rank, standing, or influence to change the course of events or get what one wants

Chapter 21

rankled: (verb) was irritated, annoyed, in this usage upset enough to have the fur stand on end

accusation: (noun) charge of guilt or blame placed on someone; to accuse of wrongdoing

"throw the book at you": (idiom) referring to a book of law and giving out or throwing every possible punishment in the book at a criminal; not just making sure justice is done but using every law and rule available to punish someone

disdain: (noun) contempt, scorn, and disgust; seeing something as vile and awful

proclaimed: (verb) announced, stated, or declared in a formal and official way

promotions: (noun) chances for advancements or achieving the next steps in ranks or jobs

Chapter 22

atmosphere: (noun) mood, feeling, or ambience of the environment or surrounding area

"have eyes on": (idiom) to be able to see and keep track of something or someone; having made visual contact with someone or something

indication: (noun) clue, hint, sign, or evidence

Chapter 23

exasperation: (noun) frustration, disbelief, irritation, or annoyance

indignities: (noun) humiliating treatments; acts that offend body or mind; losses of dignity

swaddled: (verb) wrapped up tightly, like an infant in a blanket

Mr. Tumnus: (noun) a faun character from the book *The Lion, the Witch and the Wardrobe* by C. S. Lewis

adoration: (noun) devoted love, worship, and strong admiration

Chapter 24

retrieval: (noun) recapture, bring back, recover, or restore; reclaiming something that was lost or missing and restoring it to its rightful place

outrageous: (adj.) wild, crazy, unwise, or ridiculous

Salem Witch Trails: (noun/event) trials held in Salem, Massachusetts, in 1692-1693, to prove that some individuals were witches, universally considered to be false accusations of innocent people, and often included animals like dogs or cats, who were also associated with witchcraft

massacres: (noun) unnecessary and widespread killings, usually of innocent people or animals

About the Author

Meg Dendler has considered herself a writer since she won a picture book contest in fifth grade and entertained her classmates with ongoing sequels for the rest of the year. Beginning serious work as a freelancer in the 1990s while teaching elementary and middle school, Meg has more than one hundred articles in print, including interviews with Kirk Douglas, Sylvester Stallone, and Dwayne "The Rock" Johnson. She has won contests with her short stories and poetry, along with multiple international awards for her best-selling "Cats in the Mirror" alien rescue cat children's book series. *Bianca: The Brave Frail and Delicate Princess* was named Best Juvenile Book of 2018 by the Oklahoma Writers' Federation.

Meg and her family live in Arkansas.

Visit her at www.megdendler.com for more information about upcoming books and events and all of Meg's social media links.

Made in the USA
Columbia, SC
14 April 2023